THIRTY POEMS BY ROBERT BROWNING

Books by **W. S. Mackie**

★

FIFTY COMPREHENSION TESTS
FIFTY CERTIFICATE COMPREHENSION TESTS

THIRTY POEMS BY ROBERT BROWNING

EDITED WITH INTRODUCTION AND NOTES

BY

W. S. MACKIE

FORMERLY PROFESSOR OF ENGLISH LANGUAGE IN THE UNIVERSITY OF CAPE TOWN

Macmillan Education

First edition 1949.
Reprinted 1950, 1962, 1965 (twice), 1967 (twice)
1968, 1971 (twice), 1972, 1974, 1977 (twice), 1981

Published by
MACMILLAN EDUCATION LTD
*Houndmills Basingstoke Hampshire RG21 2XS
and London
Associated companies in Delhi Dublin
Hong Kong Johannesburg Lagos Melbourne
New York Singapore and Tokyo*

ISBN 0 333 01543 6

*Printed in Hong Kong by
Dah Hua Printing Press Co., Ltd.*

CONTENTS

INTRODUCTION	- - - - -	vii
1. CAVALIER TUNES	- - - -	1
2. HOW THEY BROUGHT THE GOOD NEWS FROM GHENT TO AIX	- - -	5
3. HERVÉ RIEL	- - - - -	9
4. ECHETLOS	- - - - -	17
5. THE PIED PIPER OF HAMELIN	- -	20
6. THE POPE AND THE NET	- - -	32
7. SIBRANDUS SCHAFNABURGENSIS	- -	35
8. CHILDE ROLAND TO THE DARK TOWER CAME	- - - - -	39
9. THE LABORATORY	- - - -	49
10. MY LAST DUCHESS	- - - -	52
11. PORPHYRIA'S LOVER	- - -	55
12. THE PATRIOT	- - - -	58
13. THE LOST LEADER	- - - -	60
14. THE GRAMMARIAN'S FUNERAL	- -	62
15. THE BISHOP ORDERS HIS TOMB AT SAINT PRAXED'S CHURCH	- - -	70
16. PICTOR IGNOTUS	- - - -	76
17. A TOCCATA OF GALUPPI'S	- - -	80
18. HOME THOUGHTS, FROM ABROAD	-	85
19. DE GUSTIBUS—	- - - -	86
20. UP AT A VILLA—DOWN IN THE CITY	-	89
21. TIME'S REVENGES	- - - -	94
22. YOUTH AND ART	- - - -	97
23. LOVE AMONG THE RUINS	- - -	101
24. THE FLOWER'S NAME	- - -	105

v

25. MEETING AT NIGHT. PARTING AT
         MORNING - - - - - - 107
26. A WOMAN'S LAST WORD - - - 109
27. ONE WAY OF LOVE - - - - 112
28. POETICS - - - - - - 113
29. HOUSE - - - - - - 114
30. EPILOGUE TO *Asolando* - - - - 117
SHORT BIBLIOGRAPHY - - - - - 119
INDEX OF FIRST LINES - - - - 120

INTRODUCTION

ROBERT BROWNING, like so many other great English poets, was a Londoner, born in Camberwell on 7th May, 1812. His father was a senior clerk in the Bank of England, his mother the daughter of a German ship-owner who had settled in Dundee and married a Scotswoman. He was very fortunate in his parents. His mother was a gentle pious lady with quiet musical tastes; her son's semi-orthodox Christianity, and his interest in music and wide knowledge of its composers (shown, for example, in *A Toccata of Galuppi's*), no doubt largely derive from her influence. The elder Robert Browning was an amateur scholar and artist who collected pictures and books ; he had over 6000 volumes in his library. A kind and indulgent father, he had a love for quaint and out-of-the-way fields of knowledge which his son amply inherited.

Browning sprang, then, from the educated middle class in the English social hierarchy. All through his life he practised what have been called " the solid middle-class virtues ". Intellectually he was a man of wide understanding and tolerance, who could find something of good even in things evil, and excuses for " the meanest of God's creatures ". But in the conduct of his own life he was almost a model of robust respectability, with a healthy enough distaste for moral irregularities, or for the eccentric posturings of any out-at-elbows artistic clique, or for the " scented poetry " of Rossetti and his school. In his political views he was a Liberal and a Reformer. He grew up in the period of the aftermath of the French Revolution, and imbibed the ideas of " liberty, equality, and fraternity " that it had blazed abroad over a shaken world. He wrote a sonnet entitled " Why I am a Liberal ", and the attitude expressed in *The Lost Leader* was certainly his own. In his later years, indeed, as is quite common, his Liberalism became not only old-fashioned but somewhat timid, so that he was an opponent of Gladstone's Home Rule bill and showed other signs of satisfaction with things as they are. But an enthusiasm for human freedom constantly shines out in his poetry.

He attended two schools in his boyhood, but his education was mainly at home and from his father, who inspired him with a delight in learning and then encouraged his study of whatever aroused his interest. He learnt, of course, Latin and Greek ; and in one of his latest poems, *Development*, he describes the way in which his father tried to explain to him, when only five years old, what was meant by the siege of Troy.

> He piled up chairs and tables for a town,
> Set me a-top for Priam, called our cat
> Helen, enticed away from home (he said)
> By wicked Paris, who couched somewhere close
> Under the foot-stool, being cowardly.

He read omnivorously in his father's library, and stored all kinds of miscellaneous knowledge in his retentive memory, knowledge that later he too often worked allusively into his poems, to the mystification of his bewildered readers. It would seem to have been his mother who implanted in him his love of flowers and gardens, and, as *Sibrandus Schafnaburgensis* well shows, he took a characteristic delight in watching the quaint and varied insect life that crawls or buzzes in these.

The boy's reading of English poetry naturally led him to write verses of his own, imitations of Byron and other favourite authors which he fondly imagined to be original, and at the early age of thirteen he had put together a volume entitled *Incondita*, for which his admiring father was fortunately unable to find a publisher. In 1826 he bought a pirated edition of the lyrics of Shelley, whose greatness as a poet was only then beginning to be recognised. He was captivated by them; and no other English poet had a greater influence upon him. The varied metres of his poems, for example, seem often to be consciously or unconsciously drawn from Shelley. It was in Shelleyan blank verse that his earliest published work, *Pauline*, was composed. It appeared in 1833, and had favourable notices from critics, although not a single copy was sold. It is very unlike Browning's later works in being self-revealing, the confessions of an adolescent, and in being rather morbid in tone. In after years he himself thoroughly disapproved of it; " it is altogether foolish," he wrote Elizabeth Barrett, " ambiguous, feverish "; and when he allowed it to be republished in 1868 it was " with extreme reluctance ". His condemnation of it is understandable but not wholly deserved; it is a formless, rambling poem, but has passages of real poetic beauty. " Unripe fruit," said a contemporary critic very justly, " but of flavour and promise."

Ever encouraged by his father, and undeterred by the failure of *Pauline*, Browning resolved to make poetry his career and life's work. So in 1835 appeared *Paracelsus*. A poem in blank verse and in five parts, its theme is the insufficiency of the intellect alone in the conduct of life. It is characteristic of Browning that his embodiment of this theme is, historically, an almost forgotten German physician, an eager and quarrelsome Renaissance figure, of the early sixteenth century. The poem is too long drawn out, but a little determination will find it quite readable ; and it contains three fine lyrics that already show where Browning's strength as a poet really lies.

Paracelsus made no great appeal to the ordinary reading public, but it gained favourable reviews, made its author known, and brought him into the literary circles of the day. Descriptions of him as a young man have consequently come down to us. He was of middle height, " slim and dark ", with a handsome face framed in the long hair and luxuriant whiskers which were the flamboyant fashion of the time. He had a resonant voice—" they all say here that I speak too loud ", he confesses ruefully in a letter to Elizabeth Barrett—and was " a trifle of a dandy ", writes a lady on whom he called, " addicted to lemon-coloured kid-gloves and such things ". She adds that he was full of ambition, eager for fame, and determined to achieve success. He certainly had the precious gift of making people like him by being his own natural self. He was a lively, though in later years a rather overwhelming, conversationalist ; but above all he had the charm of a frank and open nature, readily appreciative of good work or good qualities in others, and very free from any kind of pettiness or malice. A lasting friendship that he made at this time was with Thomas Carlyle, and that censorious Scotsman was not warm-hearted towards anyone second-rate in intellect or character. Yet Browning had a fiery temper which would break out in what we should now think un-dignified splutterings at any real or imagined slight or wrong. The Victorians, however, were in general less averse to emotional scenes than are their more reticent descendants.

One of Browning's friendships was with the actor Macready, who, much impressed by *Paracelsus*, gave him the welcome advice to attempt a play. The result was the historical drama *Strafford*, on the ill-fated minister of Charles the First, which was produced at Covent Garden Theatre in May, 1837. Two others of his seven plays, *A Blot in the 'Scutcheon* (1843) and *Colombe's Birthday* (1853) appeared on the contemporary stage. His experiences with the theatre and actors—" that rouged, wigged, padded, empty-headed, heartless tribe of grimacers ", he exclaims splenetically in a letter to Elizabeth Barrett—were far from happy, and by the time that *A Blot in the 'Scutcheon* was produced his relations with Macready were stormy. His plays could not be stage successes, and are not among his best work. It is curious that a poet who could present character so vividly in lyric or monologue could yet not deal effectively with the interaction of character upon character which a play requires. With the exception of *Colombe's Birthday* all are remorselessly tragic, flash-lit neither by the satiric humour of *The Bishop Orders his Tomb* nor by the sardonic grimness of *The Laboratory*. Like the plays of Tennyson, they may be put into the category of estimable works that need not be read.

In 1840 Browning published *Sordello*, a narrative poem in rhymed couplets, its story taken from a confused period of medieval Italian history. It greatly damaged his growing reputation ; both critics and readers found it unintelligible, and the time had not yet come when crabbed obscurity in a poem would be regarded as a virtue. The darkness of *Sordello* threw its shadow on the reception of Browning's next work, *Pippa Passes* (1841). Yet it is the most beautiful and memorable of his longer poems, and is written in a style which with rare exceptions is almost limpidly clear. " I like it ", wrote Browning himself to Elizabeth Barrett, " better than anything else I have done yet." The strikingly original scheme of the poem flashed into his mind when he was walking in the woods near Dulwich. It is in dramatic form, and consists of a series of unrelated scenes, linked together by the passing by in each of Pippa. She is an Italian work-girl, who, on a day's holiday, wanders along the country-side, singing songs that have a profound and purifying effect upon men and women at emotional crises in their lives. Browning had made his first visit to Italy in 1838, and the poem illustrates his close and keen observation of Italian life and scenery. The shortest of Pippa's songs is the most famous.

> The year's at the spring
> And day's at the morn ;
> Morning's at seven ;
> The hill-side's dew-pearled ;
> The lark's on the wing ;
> The snail's on the thorn ;
> God's in his heaven—
> All's right with the world.

The last two lines have often been snatched from their context and quoted as a blatant example of Browning's " blind optimism "—a blind mistake, since it does not see that they are dramatic, depend on the lines that precede, and simply express the hopeful happiness of an Italian girl on holiday in the sunshine of a perfect morning.

Pippa Passes was published as the first of a series of paper-clad volumes for which Browning found in *Exodus* 28, 33 the quaint title of *Bells and Pomegranates*, denoting, he afterwards explained, a " mixture of music with discoursing, sound with sense, poetry with thought ". The second volume was one of his plays, the third, published late in 1842, was *Dramatic Lyrics*, and *Dramatic Romances and Lyrics* came after three more plays in 1845. He had at last discovered the type of poetry that gave the fullest and best expression to his genius.

The dramatic lyric contrasts with the personal lyric. In the personal lyric, such as Shelley's *Ode to the West Wind*, the poet expresses his own feelings. In the

dramatic lyric the poet first imagines a situation—
Cavaliers marching to battle, riders bringing good
news from Ghent, the lover awaiting his lady—and
then seeks to express the feelings which this situation
would arouse in the principal actor or actors in it.
Browning popularised the name, but in fact this type
of lyric is as old as the beginnings of English poetry.
Nearly all the Old English lyrics belong to it, many of
the medieval ballads, and in later times all the best
lyrics of Sir Walter Scott. It was a form of poetry
which admirably suited Browning, since in it he could
combine his insight into human character and his
power of expressing passion passionately. He pro-
ceeded from it to the dramatic monologue, of which
The Bishop Orders his Tomb is an outstanding example.
In this the lyric element is absent, and the poem simply
becomes a dramatic representation or exposure of the
speaker's personality from his own mouth. This again
was nothing absolutely new in English poetry ;
Chaucer had done the same, and with equal success,
in his *Prologue to the Wife of Bath's Tale*. But the
dramatic monologues of Browning have a tang of
absolute originality that makes the best of them his
most individual contribution to English literature.
" I only make men and women speak," he wrote
modestly to Elizabeth Barrett, " give you truth
broken into prismatic hues, and fear the pure white
light."

His courtship and marriage of Elizabeth Barrett was
the greatest adventure of Browning's life. Born in
1806, she was one of the large family of Edward

Moulton Barrett, the owner of estates in the West Indies and a business in London. A riding accident when she was a girl damaged her health, and she lived a semi-invalid in her own rooms in her father's house in Wimpole Street, where her charm and bright intelligence gathered a circle of friends round her. She had published several books of verse, including a translation of a Greek play, before the romantic sensibility of her *Poems*, published in two volumes in 1844, appealed to the taste of the age and brought her fame. The American poet Edgar Allan Poe dedicated a book of poems to her as to " the noblest of her sex ". " Sir," she replied with ironical wit, " you are the most discerning of yours."

The *Poems* included the overflowing *Lady Geraldine's Courtship*, " a romance of the age " in which a great lady chooses a petulant young poet as her husband. One of the stanzas praises Browning alongside of Wordsworth and Tennyson.

> Or at times a modern volume—Wordsworth's solemn-thoughted idyll,
> Howitt's ballad-verse, or Tennyson's enchanted reverie,
> Or from Browning some " Pomegranate ", which, if cut deep down the middle,
> Shows a heart within blood-tinctured, of a veined humanity.

Highly pleased by this compliment, Browning wrote his first letter to his future wife in January 1845, beginning, most happily, " I love your verses with all my heart, dear Miss Barrett." Correspondence led to acquaintance, and acquaintance to love, explosively sudden on his part, becoming a steady glow on hers. Their story has recently become widely known through the success on stage and screen of Rudolf Besier's play *The Barretts of Wimpole Street*. His telling of it is generally accurate, although Edward Moulton Barrett was not quite so monstrous a ghoul as he (and Charles Laughton) represented him to be. He was, however, almost an embodiment of the popular idea of a Victorian father, a sanctimonious and temperamental domestic tyrant, whose " heaviest displeasure " was easily aroused ; moreover, he had a determination near to monomania that, if he could help it, none of his daughters should marry and so pass outside his control. " If a prince of El Dorado should come, with a pedigree of lineal descent from some signory in the moon in one hand, and a ticket of good behaviour from the nearest Independent chapel in the other— ' Why, even then ', said my sister Arabel, ' it would not do.' " Browning is generally looked upon as a Childe Roland who stormed the Dark Tower and rescued its imprisoned princess ; but when one reads the astonishing series of love-letters that passed between them (published by their son in 1899), one must admire the intuitive skill with which Elizabeth Barrett managed her impetuous and impulsive lover. On a September morning in 1846 the two were secretly married in Marylebone Church, and a week later, with her faithful maid Wilson and her dog Flush, she left her father's house for ever and went to Italy with her husband. " So ", said Wordsworth, " Robert Browning and Miss Barrett have gone off together. I hope

they understand each other—nobody else would."
He himself, it would appear, had not failed to understand *The Lost Leader*.

After a short stay in Pisa they settled in large cool
rooms in Florence, their home for fourteen years.
They made lengthy excursions from it, including three
visits to Paris and London. Their only son, usually,
from his childish nickname, known as " Pen " Browning, was born in March 1849. In Italy and in happiness
Mrs. Browning's health at first greatly improved; " it
seems like a dream ", she writes, " when I find myself
able to climb the hills with Robert, and help him to
lose himself in the forests." Theirs was an ideal
union, notwithstanding some disagreements ; Mrs.
Browning's credulous interest in spiritualism, for
instance, caused some annoyance to her husband, who
saw through its shams and trickeries, and later exposed
these in *Mr. Sludge the Medium*. They inspired each
other to his and her best work, but were careful to
write quite independently, and keep to their own
different styles. Mrs. Browning's passionate *Sonnets
from the Portuguese* has the stamp of permanence ; her
Aurora Leigh, a novel in blank verse, with a hero who
is a monument of Victorian priggishness, although
very popular in its day, and considered " advanced ",
has not stood the test of time nearly so well. Browning
himself published, in 1850, *Christmas Eve and Easter
Day*, in which he made his first appearance as a Christian
philosopher. The best part of it is its pungently
realistic description of a Nonconformist Little Bethel
in the London slums, and of its grotesque congrega-

tion who listened entranced to " the preaching man's immense stupidity ".

> My old fat woman purred with pleasure,
>   And thumb round thumb went twirling faster,
> While she, to his periods keeping measure,
>   Maternally devoured the pastor.

In 1855 appeared his masterpiece, *Men and Women*, a wonderful collection of dramatic lyrics and mono- logues into which he put all his strength and ori- ginality. It was, as usual, received with acclamation by the few and neglect by the many ; in one of her letters his wife justly complains of " the blindness, deafness, and stupidity " of the English public towards her husband's work. The last poem, *One Word More*, is his beautiful dedication of the volume to his wife— " yourself my moon of poets " ; and *By the Fireside* contains the small vivid picture of her

> Reading by firelight, that great brow
>   And the spirit-small hand propping it,
> Yonder, my heart knows how.

During 1860 Mrs. Browning's precarious health began to fail, and she died, a victim of phthisis, in June 1861. When the first shock of separation and loneliness was over, Browning determined to leave Italy. " I shall try to work hard," he wrote to his sister Sarianna, " educate my son, and live worthy of my past fifteen years' happiness." Returning to London, he bought a house in Warwick Crescent, off Harrow Road to the north of Hyde Park. It was his home for most of the rest of his life, and his sister joined him there after the death of their father in 1866.

His correspondence with Miss Isa Blagden, who lived in Florence and was a close friend of his wife's, went on until her death in 1873, and gives us much information about him. In the summers of 1862 and 1863 he went to Pornic, in the south of Brittany, and this seaside town and the country round it, " solitary and bare enough ", make several appearances in *Dramatis Personae* (1864). This is a worthy sequel to *Men and Women*, although some of the poems in it have a bleakness that is new in his work. The younger generation, particularly at Oxford and Cambridge, were now becoming aware of Browning—" all my new cultivators ", he wrote, " are young men "—and *Dramatis Personae* was the first of his books to run into a second edition.

He was now busy with what he intended to be his *magnum opus*. In Florence in 1860 he had picked up at a book-stall " an old yellow book ", containing contemporary accounts of the trial and conviction in Rome in 1698 of Count Guido Franceschini for the murder of his wife and her parents. This is the source of *The Ring and the Book*, published in four volumes in 1868 and 1869. Its very original scheme was planned by Browning when he was holidaying in the Pyrenees in 1864. It tells the same story from the points of view of nine different people—the principal actors in it, street gossips, the lawyers, the Pope. It is a series of lengthy dramatic monologues, in which the speakers lay bare their thoughts, feelings, motives, or, as Browning would have said, their souls. The poem firmly and finally established his rapidly growing reputation. The Victorians believed that a major poet should write a major poem, and here was one before them, of 21,000 lines and more. The reviews were enthusiastic. "It is", said the *Athenaeum*, "the most precious and profound spiritual treasure that England has produced since the days of Shakespeare." As this indicates, what our great-grandparents admired was not so much Browning the poet as Browning the preacher. Solemn essays on his "message" began to appear; and "In the words of that great Christian moralist Robert Browning" became the approximate beginning of many a sermon. The poem appealed to the age because the moral sentiments and attitudes glorified in it are as mid-Victorian as those declaimed by Tennyson in the *Idylls of the King*. Nowadays it is famous and neglected. Its inordinate length appals us, even though, according to Browning, "it is the shortest poem, for the stuff in it, I ever wrote". Its cleverness, its insight into humanity, even its sustained flashes of noble poetry, do not save it from tedium, and it has become an unread classic. As Mr Clifford Bax has said, it is no longer "tense enough to grip".

Browning enjoyed his success, and had no objection to being lionised. He plunged into Society, accepted invitations, and, like Thackeray, became a member of the fashionable world, an assiduous diner-out and a guest at country-house parties. This metamorphosis was not altogether to the liking of some of his older friends : "Browning", growled Tennyson, "will die in a dress-suit." We have his own uneasy apology in a letter to Miss Blagden in 1870. "I suppose it is a gain in some respects to the soul to have seen so many people ; I mainly care about human beings ; yet I feel weary of the crowd I chose to fancy it would do me good to see ; and only get an ignoble touch of satisfaction when I think that it riles such a filthy little snob as Mr Alfred Austin to read in the *Morning Post* how many dinners I eat in good company." His fame as a poet, his exciting talk, his sense of fun, and his complete lack of conceit and affectation made him a guest much sought after. His method of escaping from a bore at any party or reception, by means of a genial " But, my dear fellow, I am monopolising you ", was both courteous and effective. He especially liked the society of sympathetic women, with whom he was always, and sometimes unwisely, less reserved than with men, as indeed his letters show.

Possibly his desire for social advancement, more certainly the expense of his new way of life, and above all his anxiety about the future of his son, who had grown up a pleasant and rather ineffective young man with no great capacity for making his own living, led Browning in 1872 to make an unfortunate blunder. One of his friends among the great was Lady Ashburton, whose husband had died in 1864. She was a mature beauty of the dark majestic type, who had intelligence, social prestige, and wealth and landed estates. While on a visit to her house in Scotland Browning made her a proposal of marriage. As it would seem that he honestly but tactlessly told her his real reasons, and also gave her to understand that his heart was buried in Florence, it is not surprising that the lady rejected his suit with the indignation of injured vanity. It was the end of their friendship; Browning afterwards believed that she had spread unkind and untrue stories about him; and much later, in 1887, he remembered her when drawing an uncomplimentary picture of "a bold she-shape briskmarching", bending "no inch of her imperious stature", in his *Parleying with Daniel Bartoli*. The incident brought him only annoyance and regret, and his feeling that he had proved unfaithful to the memory of his wife may be dimly traced under dramatic disguises in one or two of his later works.

His gyrations in good society did not diminish Browning's productivity, and during the eighteen-seventies he published, on an average, a book a year. But now there are more nettles than corn. *Prince Hohenstiel-Schwangau* (1871) and *Fifine at the Fair*, (1872), for example, are arid intellectual exercises, studies in sophistry, in which the light of poetry shines only in fitful and smoky flashes. In both Browning takes and enjoys the role of defending counsel, making out a specious case in the first for the political adventurer, and in the second for the sensualist. His interest in crime and criminals led him to write in blank verse two "sensation novels", as Swinburne called them. *Red Cotton Nightcap Country* (1873) shambles drearily along, and is remembered only for its quaint title. He took more pains over *The Inn Album* (1875), a tense melodrama with stagy characters and superheated emotions. Browning had always a weakness for melodrama; it goes with his love for flaring colours in his descriptions and explosive surprises in his style. In the two series of *Dramatic Idyls* (1879 and 1880) we have once again dramatic lyrics and monologues, at least two of which, *Pheidippides* and *Echetlos*, both on Greek subjects, will stand comparison with his earlier work. *Pacchiarotto* (1876) includes poems that are more undisguisedly personal than usual. In *At the 'Mermaid'* and *House*, for example, he vigorously asserts his determination to keep his own private thoughts and feelings away from the stare of curious onlookers. Making Shakespeare speak in the first of these, he writes,

> Which of you did I enable
>   Once to slip inside my breast,
> There to catalogue and label
>   What I like least, what love best,
> Hope and fear, believe and doubt of,
>   Seek and shun, respect, deride?
> Who has right to make a rout of
>   Rarities he found inside?

Pacchiarotto, the poem which gives its name to the book, is a rattle of grotesque rhymes (e.g. *ranunculus* with *Tommy-make-room-for-your-uncle us*) ending in robustious abuse of his less intelligent critics, notably Alfred Austin, a criticaster and poeticule of the time who had made himself Browning's pet aversion.

During the last part of his life he regularly spent the winter and spring in his home in London and the summer and early autumn abroad, in France or Switzerland or Italy. He had no longer any real anxiety about his son, who was becoming a fairly successful artist and sculptor. His own fame continued to grow, and he was glorified by admirers as the " Chief Poet of his Age ". Honorary degrees were conferred upon him by the Universities of Oxford, Cambridge, and Edinburgh. At the Oxford ceremony a wicked undergraduate in the gallery neatly dropped a red cotton nightcap on his head, to the horror of the authorities and his own hearty amusement. In 1881, largely owing to the efforts of a distinguished and excitable scholar, Dr Furnivall, the Browning Society was formed, and devoted itself to the interpretation of his works and the publication of commentaries upon them. He was gratified by this tribute, and sensibly aware of the stimulating effect which the Society had upon the sale of his books, but sometimes a little embarrassed by the " overknowingness " of its members and the mild ridicule which some of their antics excited. " The Browning Society," he writes in 1882, " as well as Browning himself, are fair game for criticism. I had no more to do with the founding it than the babe unborn, and . . . I am quite other than a Browningite. . . . That there is a grotesque side to the thing is certain, but I have been surprised and touched by what cannot but have been well-intentioned." The Society, however, did valuable service in obtaining from the poet himself explanations of obscure or ambiguous passages in his works. The last five years of his life were the St. Martin's summer of his poetry. There are fine things in *Jocoseria* (1883) and *Ferishtah's Fancies* (1884), but it is particularly in his last volume, *Asolando* (1889), that we find poems reminiscent of the freshness and vitality of his earlier and best work.

Its jewelled love-lyrics, even though the poetry of compliment rather than of passion, are remarkable from a man now over seventy years of age. One of them, *Poetics*, is included in the present volume.

In 1887 Browning was made happy by his son's marriage to Fannie Coddington, a pretty American girl who at once gained his warmest affection—" my daughter in love and law, . . . good, true, sympathetic in every way." In this year, however, his health, hitherto robust, began to decline. He became easily tired, and for the first time dreaded the discomforts of travel. In July 1889 he was " made quite ill " by an outburst resembling that of a quiescent volcano. A careless editor of the private letters of Edward Fitz-Gerald, the author of the *Rubaiyat of Omar Khayyam*, who had died in 1883, allowed a brutally unsympathetic reference to Elizabeth Barrett Browning and her *Aurora Leigh* to pass into print. Browning read it in Italy, and his impulsive wrath broke out in a bitterly vituperative sonnet, *To Edward FitzGerald*, which he sent to the editor of the *Athenaeum*. A few days later he regretted what he had done, and sent a cancelling telegram, which the editor, with an eye to the literary sensation that would ensue, was unscrupulously careful not to open until the sonnet was published. " I felt it ", said Browning in apologetic reply to remonstrances, " as if she had died yesterday."

In November 1889 he went on a visit to his son and daughter-in-law in Venice. A cold developed into bronchitis, and on the twelfth of December, the day on which *Asolando* was published, he died peacefully from heart-failure. His body was taken to England and buried in the Poets' Corner in Westminster Abbey. The third stanza of the *Epilogue* to *Asolando*, probably the last poem he wrote, is his true and noble epitaph.

The excellence of Browning's earlier lyrics and monologues, from *Dramatic Lyrics* of 1842 to *Dramatis Personae* of 1864, makes one surprised at the coldness with which they were at first received by the reading public of their time. They were too novel and original to meet with immediate favour. They were, indeed, startlingly different from what the general taste of the age expected poetry to be. They were not sentimentally romantic, their rhythms were not soothingly mellifluous, and their style was neither limpid nor luscious. They often treated strange themes in a strange way, and serious themes with an uncomfortable realism. Like every great original writer, Browning had himself to create the taste to which his work would appeal. His adventurous vocabulary, hospitable to any word or phrase that would suit his purpose, his turbulent syntax, investing conversational idiom with a new excitement, his unusual verse-forms, each admirably suited to the theme and tone of its poem—in fact, just those individual qualities of his work which now stimulate and delight us aroused in those days a horrified shudder. " His words can't and won't run straight ", complains a contemporary critic ; " a hitch and a sharp crook in every sentence bring us up with a shock." He goes on to compare Browning's style to zigzag lightning—a not inappropriate image, since Browning is one of the great impressionists in English poetry. He describes, for example, not with the exquisite detail that we often find in Tennyson, but with one or two illuminating flashes :

> an English lane
> By a cornfield-side a-flutter with poppies,

or,

> You've the brown ploughed land before, where the oxen steam and wheeze,
> And the hills over-smoked behind by the faint grey olive-trees.

In his best work he is one of the most vivid and least abstract of English poets. He at once transmutes an idea into the appropriate image, and a series of images puts the theme, or the speaker, clearly before us.

His much-advertised obscurity has also been much exaggerated. There are very few " Sordello-isms ", as Mrs. Browning called them, in the thirty poems in this present volume ; most of them, indeed, are quite startlingly clear. Except for his remote allusions to the little-known the matter of his poetry is in itself not difficult to understand. His ideas are rarely subtle and never profound. But they are often enclosed by a barbed-wire fence ; it is their expression that needs effort to penetrate. His explosive style is sometimes too fragmentary. He flashes the meaning of a whole sentence to us in a single exclamatory word or phrase, or in a brief and sudden metaphor. Thus " I certainly do not agree with you " becomes " Hoity-toity! " and " He discovered the functions of the Greek conjunction *hoti*, and there is no more to be said about it "

becomes " He settled *hoti's* business—let it be ". In
search of brevity he sometimes obscures his meaning
by taking liberties with ordinary English syntax or
idiom, as when in *Hervé Riel* " Is it merely for love or
lying? " is contorted into " Is it love the lying's for? "
In expressing a connected chain of ideas he is apt to
leap impatiently from the first to the last, and to leave
those that intervene to be supplied by the reader's
imagination or intelligence. His poetry, in short,
requires alert attention ; it is never a soothing syrup
or a restful lullaby. " I have never pretended ", he
writes in 1868, " to offer such literature as should be
a substitute for a cigar, or a game of dominoes, to an
idle man."

It is Browning's optimism, not his obscurity, that
offends our present generation. It reflects the confidence of an age that still believed that progress was
progress. But it is principally the outcome of his
sincere religious faith. Firmly believing in a future
life that would " repair what wrong earth's journeys
did ", he was keenly aware of the sins and sorrows of
this world, but too apt to sweep them from sight by a
dramatic wave of his hand towards heaven. It becomes
almost a conventional gesture ; " he relies far too
much ", writes Mr Bax, " on the word *God* when
seeking for an emotional high-light." His optimism
has not been to the taste of a disillusioned age that has
found the stoic comfort of reality in the pessimism of
Thomas Hardy. But the revulsion from it is often
mere petulance, and to be intolerant of hope and confidence is certainly not the highest wisdom.

In the selection of the thirty poems that follow I have tried to illustrate the range and variety of Browning's best work in narrative and lyric poetry. Their text is that of the standard editions, but I have occasionally modernised the punctuation. The following table gives the date and name of the magazine or volume in which each of the poems first appeared. Browning revised some of them later, but never made extensive changes.

Year	Magazine or Volume	Poems
1836	Monthly Repository (January)	Porphyria's Lover
1842	Bells and Pomegranates, III. Dramatic Lyrics	Cavalier Tunes
		The Pied Piper of Hamelin
		My Last Duchess
1844	Hood's Magazine (June)	The Laboratory
	Hood's Magazine (July)	Garden Fancies
		The Flower's Name
		Sibrandus Schafnaburgensis
1845	Hood's Magazine (March)	The Bishop Orders his Tomb
	Bells and Pomegranates, VII. Dramatic Romances and Lyrics	How they brought the Good News from Ghent to Aix
		The Lost Leader
		Pictor Ignotus
		Home Thoughts from Abroad
		Time's Revenges
		Meeting at Night and Parting at Morning

Year	Magazine or Volume	Poems
1855	Men and Women	Childe Roland to the Dark Tower Came
		The Patriot
		A Grammarian's Funeral
		A Toccata of Galuppi's
		De Gustibus—
		Up at a Villa—Down in the City
		Love among the Ruins
		A Woman's Last Word
		One Way of Love
1864	Dramatis Personae	Youth and Art
1871	Cornhill Magazine (March)	Hervé Riel
1876	Pacchiarotto	House
1880	Dramatic Idyls, 2nd Series	Echetlos
1889	Asolando	The Pope and the Net
		Poetics
		Epilogue

UNIVERSITY OF CAPE TOWN   W. S. M.
March, 1949

1. CAVALIER TUNES

(1) MARCHING ALONG

KENTISH Sir Byng stood for his King,
Bidding the crop-headed Parliament swing;
And, pressing a troop unable to stoop
And see the rogues flourish and honest folk droop,
Marched them along, fifty-score strong,
Great-hearted gentlemen, singing this song.

God for King Charles! Pym and such carles
To the Devil that prompts 'em their treasonous parles!
Cavaliers, up! Lips from the cup,
Hands from the pasty, nor bite take nor sup
Till you're—

   Chorus : Marching along, fifty-score strong,
           Great-hearted gentlemen, singing this
           song!

Hampden to hell, and his obsequies' knell
Serve Hazelrig, Fiennes, and young Harry as well!
England, good cheer! Rupert is near!
Kentish and loyalists, keep we not here

   Chorus : Marching along, fifty-score strong,
           Great-hearted gentlemen, singing this
           song!

Then, God for King Charles! Pym and his snarls
To the Devil that pricks on such pestilent carles!

Hold by the right, you double your might ;
So, onward to Nottingham, fresh for the fight,

> *Chorus :* March we along, fifty-score strong,
> Great-hearted gentlemen, singing this
> song !

(2) GIVE A ROUSE

King Charles, and who'll do him right now ?
King Charles, and who's ripe for fight now ?
Give a rouse ; here's, in hell's despite now,
King Charles !

Who gave me the goods that went since ?
Who raised me the house that sank once ?
Who helped me to gold I spent since ?
Who found me in wine you drank once ?

> *Chorus :* King Charles, and who'll do him right
> now ?
> King Charles, and who's ripe for fight
> now ?
> Give a rouse : here's, in hell's despite now,
> King Charles !

To whom used my boy George quaff else,
By the old fool's side that begot him ?
For whom did he cheer and laugh else,
While Noll's damned troopers shot him ?

> *Chorus :* King Charles, and who'll do him right
> now ?

King Charles, and who's ripe for fight
  now ?
Give a rouse : here's, in hell's despite now,
  King Charles !

(3) BOOT AND SADDLE

Boot, saddle, to horse, and away !
Rescue my castle before the hot day
Brightens to blue from its silvery grey ;

  Chorus : Boot, saddle, to horse, and away !

Ride past the suburbs, asleep as you'd say ;
Many's the friend there, will listen and pray
" God's luck to gallants that strike up the lay

  Chorus : Boot, saddle, to horse, and away ! "

Forty miles off, like a roebuck at bay,
Flouts Castle Brancepeth the Roundheads' array :
Who laughs, " Good fellows ere this, by my fay,

  Chorus : Boot, saddle, to horse, and away ? "

Who ?   My wife Gertrude ; that, honest and gay,
Laughs, when you talk of surrendering, " Nay !
I've better counsellors ; what counsel they ?

  Chorus : Boot, saddle, to horse, and away ! "

Cavalier Tunes are dramatic lyrics that refer to the Civil
War in England in the mid-seventeenth century. This was
a war between an autocratic King and a Puritan Parliament,
between Cavaliers and Roundheads. The nickname
" Roundheads " alludes to the Puritan habit of cutting

c

the hair short—hence " the crop-headed Parliament " in the first stanza of *Marching Along*. The war began when the King raised his standard at Nottingham in August 1642. After many vicissitudes the " unselfish loyalty and careless valour " of the Cavaliers were worn out by the stubborn tenacity and greater material resources of the Roundheads, and after a crushing defeat at Naseby in 1645 the King surrendered himself to a Scottish army in April 1646.

Marching Along is a song placed in the mouths of Kentish Cavaliers who at the very beginning of the war have set out to join King Charles at Nottingham. It expresses their roystering confidence in their cause and their contempt for their opponents. Pym, Hampden, Hazelrig, Fiennes, and Sir Harry Vane (" young Harry ") were prominent figures on the side of Parliament ; and Rupert is Prince Rupert of the Rhine, King Charles's nephew and the dashing leader of the Royalist cavalry.

Give a Rouse is the undaunted cry of an old Cavalier when all has been lost. In the cause of the King he has lost his house, his wealth, and his son ; but he still shouts the toast of " King Charles ", " in hell's despite ". Noll is Oliver Cromwell, whose disciplined troopers, the Ironsides, won the battles of Marston Moor and Naseby.

In *Boot and Saddle* a troop of Cavaliers are riding out from some city to relieve Castle Brancepeth, besieged by the Roundheads. There were many such sieges in the course of the Civil War.

This is the only one of the three lyrics in which Browning's telegraphic style may cause difficulty. The meaning of the last two lines of the third stanza is that someone cries laughingly that good fellows have already heard the cry " Boot, saddle, to horse, and away ". This, the last stanza tells us, is " My wife Gertrude," who scorns surrender, and is confident that rescue will come.

Carles : fellows. *Parles :* speeches. *Give a rouse :* drink a full toast. *Fay :* faith.

2. HOW THEY BROUGHT THE GOOD NEWS FROM GHENT TO AIX

I SPRANG to the stirrup, and Joris, and he ;
I galloped, Dirck galloped, we galloped all three ;
" Good speed ! " cried the watch, as the gate-bolts
    undrew ;
" Speed ! " echoed the wall to us galloping through ;
Behind shut the postern, the lights sank to rest,
And into the midnight we galloped abreast.

Not a word to each other ; we kept the great pace
Neck by neck, stride by stride, never changing our
    place ;
I turned in the saddle and made its girths tight,
Then shortened each stirrup, and set the pique right,
Rebuckled the cheek-strap, chained slacker the bit,
Nor galloped less steadily Roland a whit.

'Twas moonset at starting ; but while we drew near
Lokeren, the cocks crew and twilight dawned clear ;
At Boom, a great yellow star came out to see ;
At Düffeld, 'twas morning as plain as could be ;
And from Mecheln church-steeple we heard the half-
    chime,
So, Joris broke silence with, " Yet there is time."

At Aerschot, up leaped of a sudden the sun,
And against him the cattle stood black every one

To stare through the mist at us galloping past,
And I saw my stout galloper Roland at last,
With resolute shoulders, each butting away
The haze, as some bluff river headland its spray ;

And his low head and crest, just one sharp ear bent
  back
For my voice, and the other pricked out on his track ;
And one eye's black intelligence—ever that glance
O'er its white edge at me, his own master, askance ;
And the thick heavy spume-flakes which aye and anon
His fierce lips shook upwards in galloping on.

By Hasselt, Dirck groaned ; and cried Joris, " Stay
  spur !
Your Roos galloped bravely, the fault's not in her,
We'll remember at Aix "—for one heard the quick
  wheeze
Of her chest, saw the stretched neck and staggering
  knees
And sunk tail, and horrible heave of the flank,
As down on her haunches she shuddered and sank.

So, we were left galloping, Joris and I,
Past Looz and past Tongres, no cloud in the sky ;
The broad sun above laughed a pitiless laugh,
'Neath our feet broke the brittle bright stubble like
  chaff ;
Till over by Dalhem a dome-spire sprang white,
And " Gallop ! " gasped Joris, " for Aix is in sight ;

"How they'll greet us!"—and all in a moment his roan
Rolled neck and croup over, lay dead as a stone;
And there was my Roland to bear the whole weight
Of the news which alone could save Aix from her fate,
With his nostrils like pits full of blood to the brim,
And with circles of red for his eye-sockets' rim.

Then I cast loose my buff-coat, each holster let fall,
Shook off both my jack-boots, let go belt and all,
Stood up in the stirrup, leaned, patted his ear,
Called my Roland his pet-name, my horse without peer;
Clapped my hands, laughed and sang, any noise, bad or good,
Till at length into Aix Roland galloped and stood.

And all I remember is—friends flocking round
As I sat with his head 'twixt my knees on the ground;
And no voice but was praising this Roland of mine,
As I poured down his throat our last measure of wine,
Which (the burgesses voted by common consent)
Was no more than his due who brought good news from Ghent.

This poem, the most exciting description of a gallop in
English literature, has its scene in Flanders in the sixteenth
century. Ghent is the well-known Flemish city; Aix is
Aix-la-Chapelle or Aachen, about 110 miles to the east,
just over the frontier of Germany. Lokeren, Boom,
Aerschot, etc., are villages en route.

Browning explains in a letter of 1883, "There is no
historical incident whatever commemorated in the poem,

which I wrote . . . with a merely general impression of the characteristic warfare and besieging which abound in the annals of Flanders. This accounts for some difficulties in the time and space occupied by the ride."

The good news " which alone could save Aix from her fate " is therefore a matter for the imagination of the reader.

Good speed ! : good luck ! *Postern* : a side door or gate, not the main entrance. *Pique* : front part of the saddle. *Spume* : foam. *Croup* (pronounced *kroop*) : the hind-quarters of a horse, crupper.

3. HERVÉ RIEL

On the sea and at the Hogue, sixteen hundred ninety-
    two,
    Did the English fight the French—woe to France !
And, the thirty-first of May, helter-skelter through the
    blue,
Like a crowd of frightened porpoises a shoal of sharks
    pursue,
    Came crowding ship on ship to Saint-Malo on the
    Rance,
With the English fleet in view.

'Twas the squadron that escaped, with the victor in
    full chase ;
    First and foremost of the drove, in his great ship,
    Damfreville ;
      Close on him fled, great and small,
      Twenty-two good ships in all ;
And they signalled to the place
" Help the winners of a race.
    Get us guidance, give us harbour, take us quick—
    or, quicker still,
    Here's the English can and will ! ".

Then the pilots of the place put out brisk and leapt on
    board ;
    " Why, what hope or chance have ships like these
    to pass ? " laughed they :

Rocks to starboard, rocks to port, all the passage
    scarred and scored—
Shall the " Formidable " here, with her twelve and
    eighty guns,
   Think to make the river mouth by the single narrow
    way,
Trust to enter—where 'tis ticklish for a craft of twenty
    tons,
     And with flow at full beside ?
     Now, 'tis slackest ebb of tide.
Reach the mooring ?   Rather say,
While rock stands or water runs,
   Not a ship will leave the bay ".

Then was called a council straight.
Brief and bitter the debate :
   " Here's the English at our heels ; would you have
    them take in tow
   All that's left us of the fleet, linked together stern
    and bow,
For a prize to Plymouth Sound ?
Better run the ships aground ",
   (Ended Damfreville his speech)
" Not a minute more to wait ;
   Let the Captains all and each
   Shove ashore, then blow up, burn the vessels on
    the beach ;
France must undergo her fate.

Give the word."   But no such word
Was ever spoke or heard ;

For up stood, for out stepped, for in struck amid all
   these
—A Captain ?   A Lieutenant ?   A Mate—first,
   second, third ?
No such man of mark, and meet
With his betters to compete,
But a simple Breton sailor pressed by Tourville for
   the fleet,
   A poor coasting-pilot he, Hervé Riel the Croisickese.

And " What mockery or malice have we here ? " cries
   Hervé Riel :
   " Are you mad, you Malouins ?   Are you cowards,
      fools, or rogues ?
Talk to me of rocks and shoals, me who took the
   soundings, tell
On my fingers every bank, every shallow, every
   swell
   'Twixt the offing here and Grève where the river
      disembogues ?
Are you bought by English gold ?   Is it love the
   lying's for ?
   Morn and eve, night and day,
   Have I piloted your bay,
Entered free and anchored fast at the foot of Solidor.
   Burn the fleet and ruin France ?   That were worse
      than fifty Hogues.
      Sirs, they know I speak the truth.   Sirs, believe
         me there's a way.
Only let me lead the line,   ,
   Have the biggest ship to steer,

Get this " Formidable " clear,
Make the others follow mine,
And I lead them, most and least, by a passage I know
    well,
    Right to Solidor past Grève
      And there lay them safe and sound ;
    And if one ship misbehave,
      Keel so much as grate the ground,
Why, I've nothing but my life—here's my head," cries
    Hervé Riel.

Not a minute more to wait.
" Steer us in, then, small and great,
    Take the helm, lead the line, save the squadron,"
      cried its chief.
" Captains, give the sailor place ;
    He is Admiral, in brief."
Still the north wind, by God's grace.
See the noble fellow's face
As the big ship, with a bound,
Clears the entry like a hound,
Keeps the passage, as its inch of way were the wide
    sea's profound.
    See, safe through shoal and rock,
    How they follow in a flock,
Not a ship that misbehaves, not a keel that grates the
    ground,
    Not a spar that comes to grief :
The peril, see, is past,
All are harboured to the last,

And just as Hervé Riel hollas " Anchor ! "—sure
    as fate
Up the English come—too late.

So, the storm subsides to calm :
    They see the green trees wave
    On the heights o'erlooking Grève.
Hearts that bled are stanched with balm.
" Just our rapture to enhance
    Let the English rake the bay,
Gnash their teeth and glare askance
    As they cannonade away."
'Neath rampired Solidor pleasant riding on the Rance,
How hope succeeds despair on each Captain's coun-
    tenance.
Out burst all with one accord,
    " This is Paradise for Hell ;
      Let France, let France's King
      Thank the man that did the thing."
What a shout, and all one word,
    " Hervé Riel ! "
As he stepped in front once more,
    Not a symptom of surprise
    In the frank blue Breton eyes,
Just the same man as before.

Then said Damfreville, " My friend,
I must speak out at the end,
    Though I find the speaking hard.
Praise is deeper than the lips :
You have saved the King his ships,

You must name your own reward.
'Faith, our sun was near eclipse :
   Demand whate'er you will,
   France remains your debtor still.
   Ask to heart's content and have, or my name's not
      Damfreville."

Then a beam of fun outbroke
On the bearded mouth that spoke,
As the honest heart laughed through
Those frank eyes of Breton blue ;
" Since I needs must say my say,
   Since on board my duty's done,
   And from Malo Roads to Croisic Point, what is it
      but a run ?—
Since 'tis ask and have, I may—
   Since the others go ashore—
Come !   A good whole holiday :
   Leave to go and see my wife, whom I call the Belle
      Aurore."
That he asked and that he got—nothing more.

Name and deed alike are lost :
Not a pillar nor a post
   In his Croisic keeps alive the feat as it befell ;
Not a head in white and black
On a single·fishing-smack
In memory of the man but for whom had gone to
      wrack
   All that France saved from the fight whence England
      bore the bell.

Go to Paris : rank on rank
   Search the heroes flung pell-mell
On the Louvre, face and flank,
   You shall look long enough ere you come to Hervé
      Riel.
So, for better and for worse,
Hervé Riel, accept my verse.
In my verse, Hervé Riel, do thou once more
Save the squadron, honour France, love thy wife the
      Belle Aurore.

By this stirring narrative poem, very dramatically told, Browning has rescued the rescuer of a French fleet from semi-oblivion. It was first published in the *Cornhill Magazine* in 1871, and he gave the hundred guineas he received for it to the fund for the relief of the starving Parisians after the siege of Paris in the Franco-German War. He found the story in a local guide-book, but he misinterpreted Hervé Riel's requested reward. This was not for " a good whole holiday " but for an honourable discharge from service in the navy.

St. Malo is a seaport town on the English Channel in the east of Brittany ; in stanza 6 the pilots that board the fleet from it are called Malouins. To the south of it is Grève, at the mouth of the river Rance, up which, as far as Solidor, Hervé Riel piloted what was left of the French fleet. He himself was a native of Le Croisic, a fishing-village in the south of Brittany, near the estuary of the Loire. Tourville (stanza 3) was the admiral of the French fleet, and Damfreville the captain of the " Formidable ".

" The place " in stanza 2 is St. Malo. In stanza 6 " Is it love the lying's for ? " means " Are you talking merely for love of lying ? " In stanza 8 " Hearts that bled are stanched with balm " is a very artificial way of saying that those who were formerly in despair were now cheerful.

"Not a head in white and black" (stanza 11) means "No rough portrait". The Louvre is the famous palace and art-gallery in Paris.

Disembogues : flows into the sea. *Most and least* : both the largest and the smallest. *Stanch* : to stop bleeding, to allay. *Rampired* : fortified with ramparts.

4. ECHETLOS

HERE's a story shall stir you.   Stand up, Greeks dead
and gone,
Who breasted, beat barbarians, stemmed Persia rolling
on,
Did the deed and saved the world, for the day was
Marathon.

No man but did his manliest, kept rank and fought
away
In his tribe and file : up, back, out, down—was the
spear-arm play :
Like a wind-whipt branchy wood, all spear-arms
a-swing that day.

But one man kept no rank and his sole arm plied no
spear,
As a flashing came and went, and a form i' the van,
the rear
Brightened the battle up, for he blazed now there,
now here.

Nor helmed nor shielded he, but, a goat-skin all his
wear,
Like a tiller of the soil, with a clown's limbs broad
and bare,
Went he ploughing on and on : he pushed with a
ploughman's share.

17

Did the weak mid-line give way, as tunnies on whom
    the shark
Precipitates his bulk ?   Did the right-wing halt, when,
    stark
On his heap of slain lay stretched Kallimachos
    Polemarch ?

Did the steady phalanx falter ?   To the rescue, at the
    need,
The clown was ploughing Persia, clearing Greek earth
    of weed,
As he routed through the Sakian and rooted up the
    Mede.

But the deed done, battle won—nowhere to be
    descried
On the meadow, by the stream, at the marsh—look
    far and wide
From the foot of the mountain, no, to the last blood-
    plashed seaside,

Not anywhere on view blazed the large limbs thonged
    and brown,
Shearing and clearing still with the share before
    which—down
To the dust went Persia's pomp, as he ploughed for
    Greece, that clown.

How spake the Oracle ?   " Care for no name at all :
Say but just this : ' We praise one helpful whom we
    call

The Holder of the Ploughshare'. The great deed
ne'er grows small."

Not the great name! Sing—woe for the great name
  Miltiades
And its end at Paros isle! Woe for Themistokles,
Satrap in Sardis court! Name not the clown like these!

It was a Greek legend, told by a late writer Pausanias,
that at the battle of Marathon in 490 B.C., one of the
decisive battles in the history of the world, in which a
small Greek army routed a host of invading Persians,
a gigantic figure wielding a plough-handle could be seen
taking a valiant part in the fight. After the battle he was
seen no more. The Greeks enquired of the oracle at
Delphi, and received the reply which Browning para-
phrases in the last stanza but one.

Greek *echetlē* means " a plough-handle "; Browning has
coined *echetlos* from it but with the meaning of " the man
with the plough-share ". Kallimachos, the Polemarch or
Supreme Commander of the Greek forces, was killed in the
battle. The ablest Greek generals were Miltiades and
Themistokles. In after years Miltiades, merely in pursuit
of a private feud, made a piratical attack on the Greek
island of Paros, where he received a wound from which
he died. Themistokles had an even less creditable later
history; he was banished from Athens for corruption and
treason, and fled to the Persian court at Sardis, where he
was received with honour, but died soon afterwards. A
satrap was the governor of a Persian province, and the
Medes were a Persian, and the Sakians were a Scythian
tribe.

D

5. THE PIED PIPER OF HAMELIN

HAMELIN TOWN'S in Brunswick,
By famous Hanover city;
The river Weser, deep and wide,
Washes its wall on the southern side:
A pleasanter spot you never spied;
But, when begins my ditty,
Almost five hundred years ago,
To see the townsfolk suffer so
From vermin, was a pity.

Rats!
They fought the dogs and killed the cats,
And bit the babies in the cradles,
And ate the cheeses out of the vats,
And licked the soup from the cooks' own ladles,
Split open the kegs of salted sprats,
Made nests inside men's Sunday hats,
And even spoiled the women's chats
By drowning their speaking
With shrieking and squeaking
In fifty different sharps and flats.

At last the people in a body
To the town hall came flocking.
" 'Tis clear ", cried they, " our Mayor's a noddy;
And as for our Corporation—shocking
To think we buy gowns lined with ermine
For dolts that can't or won't determine
What's best to rid us of our vermin.

You hope, because you're old and obese
To find in the furry civic robe ease?
Rouse up, sirs. Give your brains a racking
To find the remedy we're lacking,
Or, sure as fate, we'll send you packing."
At this the Mayor and Corporation
Quaked with a mighty consternation.

An hour they sat in council,
At length the Mayor broke silence:
"For a guilder I'd my ermine gown sell,
I wish I were a mile hence.
It's easy to bid one rack one's brain—
I'm sure my poor head aches again,
I've scratched it so, and all in vain.
Oh for a trap, a trap, a trap!"
Just as he said this, what should hap
At the chamber door but a gentle tap?
"Bless us," cried the Mayor, "what's that?"
(With the Corporation as he sat,
Looking little though wondrous fat;
Not brighter was his eye, nor moister
Than a too-long-opened oyster,
Save when at noon his paunch grew mutinous
For a plate of turtle green and glutinous)
"Only a scraping of shoes on the mat?
Anything like the sound of a rat
Makes my heart go pit-a-pat."

"Come in", the Mayor cried, looking bigger;
And in did come the strangest figure.

His queer long coat from heel to head
Was half of yellow and half of red,
And he himself was tall and thin,
With sharp blue eyes, each like a pin,
And light loose hair, yet swarthy skin,
No tuft on cheek nor beard on chin,
But lips where smiles went out and in ;
There was no guessing his kith and kin :
And nobody could enough admire
The tall man and his quaint attire.
Quoth one : " It's as my great-grandsire,
Starting up at the Trump of Doom's tone,
Had walked this way from his painted tombstone."

He advanced to the council-table ;
And, " Please your Honours," said he, " I'm able,
By means of a secret charm, to draw
All creatures living beneath the sun
That creep or swim or fly or run,
After me so as you never saw ;
And I chiefly use my charm
On creatures that do people harm,
The mole and toad and newt and viper ;
And people call me the Pied Piper."
And here they noticed round his neck
A scarf of red and yellow stripe,
To match with his coat of the self-same check ;
And at the scarf's end hung a pipe ;
And his fingers, they noticed, were ever straying
As if impatient to be playing
Upon the pipe, as low it dangled

Over his vesture so old-fangled.
" Yet ", said he, " poor piper as I am,
In Tartary I freed the Cham,
Last June, from his huge swarms of gnats ;
I eased in Asia the Nizam
Of a monstrous brood of vampire-bats ;
And as for what your brain bewilders,
If I can rid your town of rats
Will you give me a thousand guilders ? "
" One ?   Fifty thousand ! "—was the exclamation
Of the astonished Mayor and Corporation.

Into the street the Piper stept,
Smiling first a little smile,
As if he knew what magic slept
In his quiet pipe the while ;
Then, like a musical adept,
To blow the pipe his lips he wrinkled,
And green and blue his sharp eyes twinkled,
Like a candle-flame where salt is sprinkled ;
And ere three shrill notes the pipe uttered
You heard as if an army muttered ;
And the muttering grew to a grumbling ;
And the grumbling grew to a mighty rumbling ;
And out of the houses the rats came tumbling.
Great rats, small rats, lean rats, brawny rats,
Brown rats, black rats, grey rats, tawny rats,
Grave old plodders, gay young friskers,
Fathers, mothers, uncles, cousins,
Cocking tails and pricking whiskers,
Families by tens and dozens,

Brothers, sisters, husbands, wives,
Followed the Piper for their lives.
From street to street he piped advancing,
And step by step they followed dancing,
Until they came to the river Weser
Wherein all plunged and perished ;
Save one who, stout as Julius Caesar,
Swam across and lived to carry
(As he, the manuscript he cherished)
To Rat-land home his commentary :
Which was, "At the first shrill notes of the pipe
I heard a sound as of scraping tripe,
And putting apples, wondrous ripe,
Into a cider-press's gripe :
And a moving away of pickle-tub-boards,
And a leaving ajar of conserve-cupboards,
And a drawing the corks of train-oil-flasks,
And a breaking the hoops of butter-casks :
And it seemed as if a voice
(Sweeter far than by harp or by psaltery
Is breathed) called out, ' Oh rats, rejoice,
The world is grown to one vast drysaltery.
So munch on, crunch on, take your nuncheon,
Breakfast, supper, dinner, luncheon ' :
And just as a bulky sugar-puncheon,
All ready staved, like a great sun shone
Glorious scarce an inch before me,
Just as methought it said, ' Come, bore me,'
—I found the Weser rolling o'er me."

You should have heard the Hamelin people

Ringing the bells till they rocked the steeple.
" Go ", cried the Mayor, " and get long poles,
Poke out the nests and block up the holes ;
Consult with carpenters and builders,
And leave in our town not even a trace
Of the rats "—when, suddenly, up the face
Of the Piper perked in the market-place,
With a " First, if you please, my thousand guilders ".

A thousand guilders !   The Mayor looked blue,
And so did the Corporation too.
For council dinners made rare havoc
With Claret, Moselle, Vin-de-Grave, Hock ;
And half the money would replenish
Their cellar's biggest butt with Rhenish.
To pay this sum to a wandering fellow
With a gipsy coat of red and yellow !
" Beside," quoth the Mayor with a knowing wink,
" Our business was done at the river's brink ;
We saw with our eyes the vermin sink,
And what's dead can't come to life, I think.
So, friend, we're not the folks to shrink
From the duty of giving you something for drink,
And a matter of money to put in your poke ;
But as for the guilders, what we spoke
Of them, as you very well know, was in joke.
Besides, our losses have made us thrifty.
A thousand guilders !   Come, take fifty."

The Piper's face fell, and he cried
" No trifling !   I can't wait, beside.

I've promised to visit by dinner-time
Bagdat, and accept the prime
Of the Head-Cook's pottage, all he's rich in,
For having left, in the Caliph's kitchen,
Of a nest of scorpions no survivor :
With him I proved no bargain-driver,
With you, don't think I'll bate a stiver ;
And folks who put me in a passion
May find me pipe after another fashion ".

" How ? " cried the Mayor, " d'ye think I brook
Being worse treated than a cook ?
Insulted by a lazy ribald
With idle pipe and vesture piebald ?
You threaten us, fellow ?   Do your worst,
Blow your pipe there till you burst ! "

Once more he stept into the street
And to his lips again
Laid his long pipe of smooth straight cane ;
And ere he blew three notes (such sweet
Soft notes as yet musician's cunning
Never gave the enraptured air)
There was a rustling that seemed like a bustling
Of merry crowds justling at pitching and hustling,
Small feet were pattering, wooden shoes clattering,
Little hands clapping and little tongues chattering,
And, like fowls in a farm-yard when barley is scattering,
Out came the children running.
All the little boys and girls,
With rosy cheeks and flaxen curls,

And sparkling eyes and teeth like pearls,
Tripping and skipping, ran merrily after
The wonderful music with shouting and laughter.

The Mayor was dumb, and the Council stood
As if they were changed into blocks of wood,
Unable to move a step, or cry
To the children merrily skipping by,
Could only follow with the eye
That joyous crowd at the Piper's back.
But how the Mayor was on the rack
And the wretched Council's bosoms beat,
As the Piper turned from the High Street
To where the Weser rolled its waters
Right in the way of their sons and daughters !
However, he turned from south to west
And to Koppelberg Hill his steps addressed,
And after him the children pressed ;
Great was the joy in every breast.
" He never can cross that mighty top ;
He's forced to let the piping drop,
And we shall see our children stop."
When, lo, as they reached the mountain-side,
A wondrous portal opened wide,
As if a cavern was suddenly hollowed ;
And the Piper advanced and the children followed,
And when all were in to the very last
The door in the mountain-side shut fast.
Did I say, all ?   No.   One was lame
And could not dance the whole of the way ;
And in after-years, if you would blame

His sadness, he was used to say,
" It's dull in our town since my playmates left ;
I can't forget that I'm bereft
Of all the pleasant sights they see
Which the Piper also promised me.
For he led us, he said, to a joyous land
Joining the town and just at hand,
Where waters gushed and fruit-trees grew
And flowers put forth a fairer hue,
And everything was strange and new ;
The sparrows were brighter than peacocks here,
And their dogs outran our fallow deer,
And honey-bees had lost their stings,
And horses were born with eagles' wings :
And just as I became assured
My lame foot would be speedily cured,
The music stopped and I stood still,
And found myself outside the hill,
Left alone against my will
To go now limping as before,
And never hear of that country more."

Alas, alas for Hamelin !
There came into many a burgher's pate
A text which says that heaven's gate
Opes to the rich at as easy rate
As the needle's eye takes a camel in.
The Mayor sent east, west, north, and south
To offer the Piper, by word of mouth,
Wherever it was men's lot to find him,
Silver and gold to his heart's content,

If he'd only return the way he went
And bring the children behind him.
But when they saw 'twas a lost endeavour,
And Piper and dancers were gone for ever,
They made a decree that lawyers never
Should think their records dated duly
If, after the day of the month and year,
These words did not as well appear,
" And so long after what happened here
On the twenty-second of July,
Thirteen hundred and seventy-six " :
And the better in memory to fix
The place of the children's last retreat,
They called it, the Pied Piper's Street,
Where anyone playing on pipe or tabor
Was sure for the future to lose his labour ;
Nor suffered they hostelry or tavern
To shock with mirth a street so solemn,
But opposite the place of the cavern
They wrote the story on a column,
And on the great church-window painted
The same, to make the world acquainted
How their children were stolen away,
And there it stands to this very day.
And I must not omit to say
That in Transylvania there's a tribe
Of alien people who ascribe
The outlandish ways and dress
On which their neighbours lay such stress,
To their fathers and mothers having risen
Out of some subterraneous prison

Into which they were trepanned
Long time ago in a mighty band
Out of Hamelin town in Brunswick land,
But how or why, they don't understand.

So, Willy, let me and you be wipers
Of scores out with all men, especially pipers ;
And whether they pipe us free fróm rats or fróm mice,
If we've promised them aught, let us keep our promise.

In *The Pied Piper of Hamelin* Browning re-tells an old
German legend. Its merry gusto, its tumbling verse that
rattles breathlessly along, its comic rhymes, and its
grotesque comparisons,

Not brighter was his eye, nor moister
Than a too-long-opened oyster,

have made it the most popular, and certainly one of the
most wholly delightful, of Browning's poems. He called
it " A Child's Story ", and it was written to amuse William
Macready, the young son of Macready the actor, who
produced two of Browning's plays.

There are several versions of the legend. The following
is the gist of that given by the English writer Verstegan
in the early seventeenth century. A piper in a fantastical
coat, hence known as the Pied Piper, undertook for a
certain sum of money to free the town of Hamelin from
the rats that infested it ; but when he had drowned all the
rats in the river Weser, the townsmen refused to pay more
than a small part of the fee that they had promised. The
piper, in revenge, enticed a hundred and thirty of the children of Hamelin by his piping into a cavern in the side of
the hill Koppelberg, and the cavern instantly closed after
them.

The allusion to Julius Caesar in the seventh stanza is to
his having to swim for his life during the fighting in Alex-

andria in 48 B.C. The Roman biographer Suetonius is the first to say that he carried documents above his head as he swam. Browning embellishes the story further by suggesting that these documents were Caesar's Commentaries, that is, the manuscripts of his books on the Gallic and Civil wars. Mr Bernard Shaw has yet again improved the tale by changing the documents into Cleopatra.

For the Biblical allusion to the camel and the needle's eye in stanza 14, see *St. Matthew* 19, verse 24.

6. THE POPE AND THE NET

WHAT, he on whom our voices unanimously ran,
Made Pope at our last Conclave ? Full low his life
 began ;
His father earned the daily bread as just a fisherman.

So much the more the boy minds book, gives proof
 of mother-wit,
Becomes first Deacon, and then Priest, then Bishop:
 see him sit
No less than Cardinal ere long, while no one cries,
 " Unfit."

But someone smirks, some other smiles, jogs elbow
 and nods head ;
Each winks at each : " I'faith, a rise ! Saint Peter's
 net, instead
Of sword and keys, is come in vogue." You think he
 blushes red ?

Not he, of humble holy heart : " Unworthy me ! "
 he sighs ;
" From fisher's drudge to Church's prince—it is
 indeed a rise ;
So, here's my way to keep the fact for ever in my
 eyes."

And straightway in his palace-hall, where commonly
 is set

Some coat-of-arms, some portraiture ancestral, lo, we
   met
His mean estate's reminder in his fisher-father's net.

Which step conciliates all and some, stops cavil in a
   trice :
" The humble holy heart that holds of new-born
   pride no spice !
He's just the saint to choose for Pope."   Each adds
   " 'Tis my advice."

So, Pope he was ; and when we flocked—its sacred
   slipper on—
To kiss his foot, we lifted eyes, alack the thing was
   gone,
That guarantee of lowlihead—eclipsed that star which
   shone.

Each eyed his fellow, one and all kept silence.   I
   cried, " Pish !
I'll make me spokesman for the rest, express the
   common wish.
Why, Father, is the net removed ? "   " Son, it hath
   caught the fish."

This witty little poem, with its amusingly cynical ending, appeared in Browning's last volume, *Asolando*, in
1889.   He may have invented the anecdote, or it may
have been told him in Italy.   Probably it was suggested
to him by the career of Sixtus the Fifth, who, though not
a fisherman's son, was born of poor parentage, and was

chosen Pope in 1585. He appears again in the succeeding poem in the same volume, *The Bean-feast*.

The first sentence means, " What, he whom our votes unanimously elected Pope at the last Conclave or Assembly of Cardinals ? "

7. SIBRANDUS SCHAFNABURGENSIS

PLAGUE take all your pedants, say I !
    He who wrote what I hold in my hand
Centuries back was so good as to die,
    Leaving this rubbish to cumber the land ;
This, that was a book in its time,
    Printed on paper and bound in leather,
Last month in the white of a matin-prime
    Just when the birds sang all together,

Into the garden I brought it to read,
    And under the arbute and laurustine
Read it, so help me grace in my need,
    From title-page to closing-line.
Chapter on chapter did I count,
    As a curious traveller counts Stonehenge ;
Added up the mortal amount ;
    And then proceeded to my revenge.

Yonder's a plum-tree with a crevice
    An owl would build in, were he but sage ;
For a lap of moss, like a fine pont-levis
    In a castle of the Middle Age,
Joins to a lip of gum, pure amber ;
    When he'd be private, there might he spend
Hours alone in his lady's chamber :
    Into this crevice I dropped our friend

Splash, went he, as under he ducked,
  —At the bottom, I knew, rain-drippings stagnate ;
Next, a handful of blossoms I plucked
  To bury him with, my bookshelf's magnate ;
Then I went in-doors, brought out a loaf,
  Half a cheese, and a bottle of Chablis ;
Lay on the grass and forgot the oaf
  Over a jolly chapter of Rabelais.

Now, this morning, betwixt the moss
  And gum that locked our friend in limbo,
A spider had spun his web across,
  And sat in the midst with arms akimbo :
So, I took pity, for learning's sake,
  And, *de profundis, accentibus laetis*,
Cantate ! quoth I, as I got a rake ;
  And up I fished his delectable treatise.

Here you have it, dry in the sun,
  With all the binding all of a blister,
And great blue spots where the ink has run,
  And reddish streaks that wink and glister
O'er the page so beautifully yellow :
  Oh, well have the droppings played their tricks !
Did he guess how toadstools grow, this fellow ?
  Here's one stuck in his chapter six.

How did he like it when the live creatures
  Tickled and toused and browsed him all over,
And worm, slug, eft, with serious features,
  Came in, each one, for his right of trover ?

When the water-beetle with great blind deaf face
   Made of her eggs the stately deposit,
And the newt borrowed just so much of the preface
   As tiled in the top of his black wife's closet?

All that life and fun and romping,
   All that frisking and twisting and coupling,
While slowly our poor friend's leaves were swamping
   And clasps were cracking and covers suppling!
As if you had carried sour John Knox
   To the play-house at Paris, Vienna or Munich,
Fastened him into a front-row box,
   And danced off the ballet with trousers and tunic.

Come, old martyr! What, torment enough is it?
   Back to my room shall you take your sweet self.
Good-bye, mother-beetle; husband-eft, *sufficit!*
   See the snug niche I have made on my shelf.
A.'s book shall prop you up, B.'s shall cover you,
   Here's C. to be grave with, or D. to be gay,
And with E. on each side, and F. right over you,
   Dry-rot at ease till the Judgement-day.

This poem and *The Flower's Name* were first published,
as *Garden Fancies*, in *Hood's Magazine* in July 1844. It is a
rollicking protest against pedantry, and records the condemnation, imprisonment, and release, " for learning's
sake ", of a monstrous monument of this, the crabbed
tome of a certain Sibrand of Aschaffenburg. " Do you
know ", wrote Elizabeth Barrett, " this poem is a great
favourite with me—it is so new, and full of a creeping
crawling grotesque life ? " It was the grotesquerie of

insects, and of toadstools, and of Rabelais, that delighted
Browning, and no other English poet could have pictured
it so well.

" The white of a matin-prime " means the white light of
mid-morning. *Stonehenge* is the ancient ring of standing-
stones on Salisbury Plain. A *pont-levis* is a drawbridge.
The *he* of line 6 of stanza 3 is the owl. The tome is " my
bookshelf's magnate " because it is the largest book in the
library. Chablis is a French wine; Rabelais the great
French writer of the early sixteenth century. " De profundis, accentibus laetis, cantate " means " Sing with joyful tones out of the depths "; it seems to be Latin of
Browning's own invention, probably suggested by " Out
of the depths have I called unto thee, O Lord " in Psalm
130. The eft or newt is a small lizard-like amphibian.
The right of trover is the right of treasure-trove, the
right to possess discovered treasure. John Knox was
the puritanical Scottish reformer of the sixteenth century.
Sufficit means " Enough ".

8. CHILDE ROLAND TO THE DARK TOWER CAME

My first thought was, he lied in every word,
   That hoary cripple, with malicious eye
   Askance to watch the working of his lie
On mine, and mouth scarce able to afford
Suppression of the glee, that pursed and scored
   Its edge, at one more victim gained thereby.

What else should he be set for, with his staff ?
   What, save to waylay with his lies, ensnare
   All travellers who might find him posted there,
And ask the road ?   I guessed what skull-like laugh
Would break, what crutch 'gin write my epitaph
   For pastime in the dusty thoroughfare,

If at his counsel I should turn aside
   Into that ominous tract which, all agree,
   Hides the Dark Tower.   Yet acquiescingly
I did turn as he pointed, neither pride
Nor hope rekindling at the end descried,
   So much as gladness that some end might be.

For, what with my whole world-wide wandering,
   What with my search drawn out through years, my
      hope
   Dwindled into a ghost not fit to cope
With that obstreperous joy success would bring,

I hardly tried now to rebuke the spring
   My heart made, finding failure in its scope.

As when a sick man very near to death
   Seems dead indeed, and feels begin and end
   The tears, and takes the farewell of each friend,
And hears one bid the other go, draw breath
Freelier outside (" since all is o'er ", he saith,
   " And the blow fallen no grieving can amend ");

While some discuss if near the other graves
   Be room enough for this, and when a day
   Suits best for carrying the corpse away,
With care about the banners, scarves, and staves :
And still the man hears all, and only craves
   He may not shame such tender love and stay.

Thus, I had so long suffered in this quest,
   Heard failure prophesied so oft, been writ
   So many times among " The Band "—to wit,
The knights who to the Dark Tower's search addressed
Their steps—that just to fail as they, seemed best,
   And all the doubt was now—should I be fit ?

So, quiet as despair, I turned from him,
   That hateful cripple, out of his highway
   Into the path he pointed.   All the day
Had been a dreary one at best, and dim
Was settling to its close, yet shot one grim
   Red leer to see the plain catch its estray.

For mark ! no sooner was I fairly found
 Pledged to the plain, after a pace or two,
 Than, pausing to throw backward a last view
O'er the safe road, 'twas gone ; grey plain all round :
Nothing but plain to the horizon's bound.
 I might go on ; nought else remained to do.

So, on I went. I think I never saw
 Such starved ignoble nature ; nothing throve :
 For flowers—as well expect a cedar grove !
But cockle, spurge, according to their law
Might propagate their kind, with none to awe,
 You'd think ; a burr had been a treasure-trove.

No! Penury, inertness, and grimace,
 In some strange sort, were the land's portion. " See
 Or shut your eyes," said Nature peevishly,
" It nothing skills ; I cannot help my case ;
'Tis the Last Judgement's fire must cure this place,
 Calcine its clods and set my prisoners free."

If there pushed any ragged thistle-stalk
 Above its mates, the head was chopped ; the bents
 Were jealous else. What made those holes and rents
In the dock's harsh swarth leaves, bruised as to baulk
All hope of greenness ? 'Tis a brute must walk
 Pushing their life out, with a brute's intents.

As for the grass, it grew as scant as hair
 In leprosy ; thin dry blades pricked the mud
 Which underneath looked kneaded up with blood.

One stiff blind horse, his every bone a-stare,
Stood stupefied, however he came there :
   Thrust out past service from the devil's stud !

Alive ?   He might be dead for aught I know,
   With that red gaunt and colloped neck a-strain,
   And shut eyes underneath the rusty mane ;
Seldom went such grotesqueness with such woe ;
I never saw a brute I hated so ;
   He must be wicked to deserve such pain.

I shut my eyes and turned them on my heart.
   As a man calls for wine before he fights,
   I asked one draught of earlier, happier sights,
Ere fitly I could hope to play my part.
Think first, fight afterwards—the soldier's art :
   One taste of the old time sets all to rights.

Not it !   I fancied Cuthbert's reddening face
   Beneath its garniture of curly gold,
   Dear fellow, till I almost felt him fold
An arm in mine to fix me to the place,
That way he used.   Alas, one night's disgrace !
   Out went my heart's new fire and left it cold.

Giles then, the soul of honour—there he stands
   Frank as ten years ago when knighted first.
   What honest man should dare (he said) he durst.
Good ! But the scene shifts. Faugh ! what hangman
     hands

Pin to his breast a parchment ? His own bands
   Read it. Poor traitor, spit upon and curst !

Better this present than a past like that ;
   Back therefore to my darkening path again !
   No sound, no sight as far as eye could strain.
Will the night send a howlet or a bat ?
I asked : when something on the dismal flat
   Came to arrest my thoughts and change their train.

A sudden little river crossed my path
   As unexpected as a serpent comes.
   No sluggish tide congenial to the glooms ;
This, as it frothed by, might have been a bath
For the fiend's glowing hoof, to see the wrath
   Of its black eddy bespate with flakes and spumes.

So petty yet so spiteful ! All along
   Low scrubby alders kneeled down over it ;
   Drenched willows flung them headlong in a fit
Of mute despair, a suicidal throng :
The river which had done them all the wrong,
   Whate'er that was, rolled by, deterred no whit.

Which while I forded,—good saints, how I feared
   To set my foot upon a dead man's cheek
   Each step, or feel the spear I thrust to seek
For hollows, tangled in his hair or beard !
It may have been a water-rat I speared,
   But ugh ! it sounded like a baby's shriek.

Glad was I when I reached the other bank.
　　Now for a better country.　Vain presage !
　　Who were the strugglers, what war did they wage
Whose savage trample thus could pad the dank
Soil to a plash ?　Toads in a poisoned tank,
　　Or wild cats in a red-hot iron cage ?

The fight must so have seemed in that fell cirque.
　　What penned them there, with all the plain to
　　　　choose ?
　　No foot-print leading to that horrid mews,
None out of it.　Mad brewage set to work
Their brains, no doubt, like galley-slaves the Turk
　　Pits for his pastime, Christians against Jews.

And more than that—a furlong on—why, there !
　　What bad use was that engine for, that wheel,
　　Or brake, not wheel—that harrow fit to reel
Men's bodies out like silk, with all the air
Of Tophet's tool, on earth left unaware,
　　Or brought to sharpen its rusty teeth of steel ?

Then came a bit of stubbed ground, once a wood,
　　Next a marsh, it would seem, and now mere earth
　　Desperate and done with—so a fool finds mirth,
Makes a thing and then mars it, till his mood
Changes and off he goes.　Within a rood
　　Bog, clay, and rubble, sand and stark black dearth.

Now blotches rankling, coloured gay and grim,
　　Now patches where some leanness of the soil's

Broke into moss or substances like boils ;
Then came some palsied oak, a cleft in him
Like a distorted mouth that splits its rim
    Gaping at death, and dies while it recoils.

And just as far as ever from the end !
    Nought in the distance but the evening, nought
    To point my footstep further !   At the thought
A great black bird, Apollyon's bosom-friend,
Sailed past, nor beat his wide wing dragon-penned
    That brushed my cap—perchance the guide I sought.

For, looking up, aware I somehow grew,
    'Spite of the dusk, the plain had given place
    All round to mountains—with such name to grace
Mere ugly heights and heaps now stolen in view.
How thus they had surprised me—solve it, you !
    How to get from them was no clearer case.

Yet half I seemed to recognise some trick
    Of mischief happened to me, God knows when—
    In a bad dream perhaps.   Here ended, then,
Progress this way.   When, in the very nick
Of giving up, one time more, came a click
    As when a trap shuts—you're inside the den.

Burningly it came on me all at once,
    This was the place.   Those two hills on the right,
    Crouched like two bulls locked horn in horn in fight,
While to the left, a tall scalped mountain. . . . Dunce,

Dotard, a-dozing at the very nonce,
    After a life spent training for the sight !

What in the midst lay but the Tower itself ?
    The round squat turret, blind as the fool's heart,
    Built of brown stone, without a counterpart
In the whole world.   The tempest's mocking elf
Points to the shipman thus the unseen shelf
    He strikes on, only when the timbers start.

Not see ?   Because of night perhaps ?   Why, day
    Came back again for that.   Before it left
    The dying sunset kindled through a cleft :
The hills, like giants at a hunting, lay,
Chin upon hand, to see the game at bay—
    " Now stab and end the creature—to the heft ! "

Not hear ?   When noise was everywhere ! it tolled
    Increasing like a bell.   Names in my ears
    Of all the lost adventurers my peers,
How such a one was strong, and such was bold,
And such was fortunate, yet each of old
    Lost, lost ! one moment knelled the woe of years.

There they stood, ranged along the hill-sides, met
    To view the last of me, a living frame
    For one more picture.   In a sheet of flame
I saw them and I knew them all.   And yet
Dauntless the slughorn to my lips I set
    And blew.   *" Childe Roland to the Dark Tower came."*

" Childe Roland to the Dark Tower came " is the first
line of a snatch of ballad spoken by Edgar, while pretend-
ing to be mad, at the end of Act III, Scene 4 of Shakespeare's
King Lear.

> Childe Rowland to the darke Tower came,
> His word was still, fie, foh, and fumme,
> I smell the blood of a British man.

This line from Shakespeare, a picture of a dreary scene in
a Paris art-gallery, the figure of a red horse in a piece of
tapestry in Browning's own house in Italy, and a squat
tower seen in the Italian mountains, were the suggestions
that set the poet's imagination to work.   The poem is a
pure fantasy, and more than once Browning stated empha-
tically that no allegorical meaning was intended.

From one point of view the poem depicts a rare type of
heroism, loyalty to a vowed purpose when both hope and
heart have alike been lost.   But its virtue lies in its descriptive power.   The nightmare landscape, with its ragged and
stunted vegetation, the gaunt hateful horse, the sudden
frothy little river, the barren blotched earth, and finally the
ugly scowling hills with the ominous Dark Tower in their
midst, are a masterpiece of imaginative word-painting.   It
is a description that should be appreciated by anyone who
has traversed the South African Karroo after a prolonged
drought.

Quests, such as this Quest of the Dark Tower, were
undertaken by Arthurian knights in medieval literature,
for example the Quest of the Holy Grail.   The parchment
pinned to Giles's breast by the hangman records his
treason.   " Tophet's tool " means an instrument of torture
such as might be used in hell.   Tophet, a valley near Jerusa-
lem, is connected in the Bible with the worship of Moloch,
a heathen god to whom human sacrifices were made. E.g.,
II *Kings*, 23, 10.   Later, the name, which means "the place
of burnings", became symbolical of the torments of hell.
" Blind as the fool's heart " is another Biblical allusion;

Psalm 14, 1 : " The fool hath said in his heart, There is no God." In the last stanza the blowing of the slughorn is the knight's challenge.

Estray : an animal that has strayed. *With none to awe :* with nothing to deter them. *It nothing skills :* it makes no difference. *Calcine :* burn up. *Bents :* stalks of coarse grass. *Colloped :* with loose folds of skin. *Howlet :* owl. *Cirque :* circle. *Mews :* stables, confined place. *At the very nonce :* at the decisive moment. *Slughorn :* a crooked ox-horn, a trumpet.

9. THE LABORATORY

ANCIEN RÉGIME

Now that I, tying thy glass mask tightly,
May gaze through these faint smokes curling whitely,
As thou pliest thy trade in this devil's smithy—
Which is the poison to poison her, prithee ?

He is with her, and they know that I know
Where they are, what they do : they believe my tears
   flow
While they laugh, laugh at me, at me fled to the drear
Empty church, to pray God in, for them—I am here.

Grind away, moisten and mash up thy paste,
Pound at thy powder—I am not in haste.
Better sit thus, and observe thy strange things,
Than go where men wait me and dance at the King's.

That in the mortar—you call it a gum ?
Ah, the brave tree whence such gold oozings come !
And yonder soft phial, the exquisite blue,
Sure to taste sweetly—is that poison too ?

Had I but all of them, thee and thy treasures,
What a wild crowd of invisible pleasures !
To carry pure death in an ear-ring, a casket,
A signet, a fan-mount, a filigree basket !

Soon, at the King's, a mere lozenge to give,
And Pauline should have just thirty minutes to live !
But to light a pastille, and Elise, with her head
And her breast and her arms and her hands, should
　　drop dead !

Quick—is it finished ?   The colour's too grim.
Why not soft like the phial's, enticing and dim ?
Let it brighten her drink, let her turn it and stir,
And try it and taste, ere she fix and prefer.

What a drop !   She's not little, no minion like me ;
That's why she ensnared him : this never will free
The soul from those masculine eyes, say, " no ! "
To that pulse's magnificent come-and-go.

For only last night, as they whispered, I brought
My own eyes to bear on her so, that I thought
Could I keep them one half-minute fixed, she would fall
Shrivelled ; she fell not ; yet this does it all.

Not that I bid you spare her the pain ;
Let death be felt and the proof remain :
Brand, burn up, bite into its grace—
He is sure to remember her dying face.

Is it done ?   Take my mask off.   Nay, be not morose ;
It kills her, and this prevents seeing it close :
The delicate droplet, my whole fortune's fee !
If it hurts her, beside, can it ever hurt me ?

Now, take all my jewels, gorge gold to your fill,
You may kiss me, old man, on my mouth if you will.
But brush this dust off me, lest horror it brings
Ere I know it—next moment I dance at the King's.

This grim study of jealous hate has its scene in France in the fifteenth or sixteenth century. It is a dramatic monologue, and is spoken by a woman who has come to the laboratory of an alchemist in order to buy poison with which to remove her rival and supplanter. The venomous irony of the second stanza, with its rapid changes of emphatic pronouns, is a particularly fine example of Browning's skill in dramatic expression.

During the Renaissance period, and especially in Italy, poisoning almost became a fine art, and had its professional practitioners. It might be suspected, but could not be detected, by the inefficient medical science of the time. From " these faint smokes curling whitely " one can gather that the poison that the alchemist is preparing is arsenic.

F

10. MY LAST DUCHESS

FERRARA

THAT's my last Duchess painted on the wall,
Looking as if she were alive.   I call
That piece a wonder, now ; Frà Pandolf's hands
Worked busily a day, and there she stands.
Will't please you sit and look at her ? I said
" Frà Pandolf " by design, for never read
Strangers like you that pictured countenance,
The depth and passion of its earnest glance,
But to myself they turned (since none puts by
The curtain I have drawn for you, but I)
And seemed as they would ask me, if they durst,
How such a glance came there ; so, not the first
Are you to turn and ask thus.   Sir, 'twas not
Her husband's presence only, called that spot
Of joy into the Duchess' cheek : perhaps
Frà Pandolf chanced to say, " Her mantle laps
Over my lady's wrist too much," or, " Paint
Must never hope to reproduce the faint
Half-flush that dies along her throat " ; such stuff
Was courtesy, she thought, and cause enough
For calling up that spot of joy.   She had
A heart—how shall I say ?—too soon made glad,
Too easily impressed ; she liked whate'er
She looked on, and her looks went everywhere.
Sir, 'twas all one.   My favour at her breast,
The dropping of the daylight in the West,
The bough of cherries some officious fool

Broke in the orchard for her, the white mule
She rode with round the terrace—all and each
Would draw from her alike the approving speech,
Or blush, at least. She thanked men—good! but
    thanked
Somehow—I know not how—as if she ranked
My gift of a nine-hundred-years-old name
With anybody's gift. Who'd stoop to blame
This sort of trifling? Even had you skill
In speech—which I have not—to make your will
Quite clear to such a one, and say, " Just this
Or that in you disgusts me; here you miss,
Or there exceed the mark ", and if she let
Herself be lessoned so, nor plainly set
Her wits to yours, forsooth, and made excuse,
E'en then would be some stooping; and I choose
Never to stoop. Oh, sir, she smiled, no doubt,
Whene'er I passed her; but who passed without
Much the same smile? This grew; I gave commands;
Then all smiles stopped together. There she stands
As if alive. Will't please you rise? We'll meet
The company below, then. I repeat,
The Count your master's known munificence
Is ample warrant that no just pretence
Of mine for dowry will be disallowed;
Though his fair daughter's self, as I avowed
At starting, is my object. Nay, we'll go
Together down, sir. Notice Neptune, though,
Taming a sea-horse, thought a rarity,
Which Claus of Innsbruck cast in bronze for me.

In *My Last Duchess*, another dramatic monologue cast in the Renaissance period, and spoken by an Italian Duke to the envoy of a Count whose daughter he is offering to marry, the ruling passion which Browning briefly but most effectively portrays is an icy, taciturn, self-centred and wholly pitiless pride. A sign of this is an irritable jealousy —" some officious fool ". The last Duchess scattered her easy smiles on whoever or whatever pleased her, instead of reserving them for her husband only, in proper appreciation of his gift of " a nine-hundred-years-old name ".

> " This grew ; I gave commands ;
> Then all smiles stopped together."

It should be observed that the Duke has the keen interest in art and sculpture characteristic of the Renaissance. Frà Pandolf and Claus of Innsbruck, however, are quite fictitious.

11. PORPHYRIA'S LOVER

THE rain set early in to-night,
  The sullen wind was soon awake,
It tore the elm-tops down for spite
  And did its worst to vex the lake:
  I listened with heart fit to break;
When glided in Porphyria; straight
  She shut the cold out and the storm,
And kneeled and made the cheerless grate
  Blaze up, and all the cottage warm;
  Which done, she rose, and from her form
Withdrew the dripping coat and shawl,
  And laid her soiled gloves by, untied
Her hat and let the damp hair fall,
  And, last, she sat down by my side
  And called me. When no voice replied
She put her arm about my waist,
  And made her smooth white shoulder bare,
And all her yellow hair displaced,
  And, stooping, made my cheek lie there,
  And spread, o'er all, her yellow hair,
Murmuring how she loved me—she
  Too weak, for all her heart's endeavour,
To set its struggling passion free
  From pride, and vainer ties dissever,
  And give herself to me for ever.
But passion sometimes would prevail,
  Nor could to-night's gay feast restrain

A sudden thought of one so pale
   For love of her, and all in vain :
   So, she was come through wind and rain.
Be sure I looked up at her eyes
   Happy and proud ; at last I knew
Porphyria worshipped me ; surprise
   Made my heart swell, and still it grew
   While I debated what to do.
That moment she was mine, mine, fair,
   Perfectly pure and good : I found
A thing to do, and all her hair
   In one long yellow string I wound
   Three times her little throat around,
And strangled her.   No pain felt she ;
   I am quite sure she felt no pain.
As a shut bud that holds a bee,
   I warily oped her lids : again
   Laughed the blue eyes without a stain
And I untightened next the tress
   About her neck ; her cheek once more
Blushed bright beneath my burning kiss :
   I propped her head up as before,
   Only, this time my shoulder bore
Her head, which droops upon it still :
   The smiling rosy little head,
So glad it has its utmost will,
   That all it scorned at once is fled,
   And I, its love, am gained instead.
Porphyria's love : she guessed not how
   Her darling one wish would be heard :
And thus we sit together now,

And all night long we have not stirred,
And yet God has not said a word !

Porphyria's Lover was first published in a magazine, the
Monthly Repository, in 1836 ; it was reprinted in *Dramatic
Lyrics*, 1842, along with another poem, *Johannes Agricola
in Meditation*, under the title *Madhouse Cells*. The closing
lines make it clear that it is a study of insanity. The lover,
believing that Porphyria is too weak to break with the
world and cry " Love is best ", tries to make one perfect
moment eternal by strangling her as she lies in his arms.
The almost matter-of-fact simplicity with which the story
is told makes its horror all the more effective.

12. THE PATRIOT

AN OLD STORY

It was roses, roses, all the way,
  With myrtle mixed in my path like mad ;
The house-roofs seemed to heave and sway,
  The church-spires flamed, such flags they had,
A year ago on this very day.

The air broke into a mist with bells,
  The old walls rocked with the crowd and cries.
Had I said, " Good folk, mere noise repels,
  But give me your sun from yonder skies,"
They had answered, " And afterward, what else ? "

Alack, it was I who leaped at the sun
  To give it my loving friends to keep.
Nought man could do, have I left undone ;
  And you see my harvest, what I reap
This very day, now a year is run.

There's nobody on the house-tops now,
  Just a palsied few at the windows set ;
For the best of the sight is, all allow,
  At the Shambles' Gate, or, better yet,
By the very scaffold's foot, I trow.

I go in the rain, and, more than needs,
  A rope cuts both my wrists behind ;

And I think, by the feel, my forehead bleeds,
  For they fling, whoever has a mind,
Stones at me for my year's misdeeds.

Thus I entered, and thus I go.
  In triumphs, people have dropped down dead.
" Paid by the world, what dost thou owe
  Me ? " God might question ; now instead
'Tis God shall repay : I am safer so.

In this tragic little poem Browning joins Chaucer and
Shakespeare in exposing the fickleness of the many-headed
multitude. Originally the Italian city Brescia was men-
tioned in the sixth stanza ; and although the story allusively told in the poem is fictitious, Browning almost
certainly had in mind some of the vicissitudes of popular
favour during the Italian struggle for freedom from
Austrian rule in 1848 and 1849.

The last stanza expresses one of his favourite ideas,
found also, for example, in *A Grammarian's Funeral*, that
apparent failure in pursuit of a high ideal may be actual
success, for

" 'Tis God shall repay : I am safer so. "

13. THE LOST LEADER

Just for a handful of silver he left us,
  Just for a riband to stick in his coat,
Found the one gift of which fortune bereft us,
  Lost all the others she lets us devote.
They, with the gold to give, doled him out silver,
  So much was theirs who so little allowed :
How all our copper had gone for his service !
  Rags—were they purple, his heart had been proud.
We that had loved him so, followed him, honoured
    him,
  Lived in his mild and magnificent eye,
Learned his great language, caught his clear accents,
  Made him our pattern to live and to die !
Shakespeare was of us, Milton was for us,
  Burns, Shelley, were with us—they watch from their
    graves.
He alone breaks from the van and the freemen,
  He alone sinks to the rear and the slaves.

We shall march prospering—not through his presence;
  Songs may inspirit us—not from his lyre ;
Deeds will be done—while he boasts his quiescence,
  Still bidding crouch whom the rest bade aspire.
Blot out his name, then, record one lost soul more,
  One task more declined, one more footpath untrod,
One more devils'-triumph and sorrow for angels,
  One wrong more to man, one more insult to God.
Life's night begins : let him never come back to us ;

There would be doubt, hesitation, and pain,
Forced praise on our part—the glimmer of twilight,
    Never glad confident morning again.
Best fight on well, for we taught him—strike gallantly,
    Menace our heart ere we master his own ;
Then let him receive the new knowledge and wait us,
    Pardoned in heaven, the first by the throne.

The theme of *The Lost Leader* was suggested to Browning by Wordsworth's defection from the liberal and even revolutionary views which he held in the " glad confident morning " of his youth, until in his later years he became, in his politics, a pillar of respectable Conservatism. Browning was always anxious to make it clear, however, that the sordid motives attributed to the Lost Leader in the poem were certainly not the motives of Wordsworth. In his own words in a letter of 1875, " I did in my hasty youth presume to use the great and venerable personality of Wordsworth as a sort of painter's model ; one from which this or the other particular feature may be selected and turned to account : had I intended ... such a boldness as portraying the entire man, I should certainly not have talked about ' handfuls of silver ' and ' bits of ribbon '. These never influenced the change of politics in the great poet ; whose defection, nevertheless, . . . was to my juvenile apprehension, and even to my mature consideration, an event to deplore."

The " riband to stick in his coat " is the decoration that denotes some honorific order or title granted by the party in power. The fourth line means, " lost all the other gifts that we are able to devote to the cause of freedom." Line 8 is a good example of Browning's habit of condensing an emotional idea in a vivid exclamation ; it means, " we had only rags to offer him, and his heart desired purple and fine linen."

14. A GRAMMARIAN'S FUNERAL

SHORTLY AFTER THE REVIVAL OF LEARNING IN EUROPE

LET us begin and carry up this corpse,
    Singing together.
Leave we the common crofts, the vulgar thorpes
    Each in its tether
Sleeping safe on the bosom of the plain,
    Cared for till cock-crow :
Look out if yonder be not day again
    Rimming the rock-row.
That's the appropriate country ; there, man's thought,
    Rarer, intenser,
Self-gathered for an outbreak, as it ought,
    Chafes in the censer.
Leave we the unlettered plain its herd and crop ;
    Seek we sepulture
On a tall mountain, citied to the top,
    Crowded with culture !
All the peaks soar, but one the rest excels ;
    Clouds overcome it ;
No !   Yonder sparkle is the citadel's
    Circling its summit.
Thither our path lies ; wind we up the heights :
    Wait ye the warning ?
Our low life was the level's and the night's ;
    He's for the morning.
Step to a tune, square chests, erect each head,
    'Ware the beholders !

This is our master, famous, calm and dead,
　　Borne on our shoulders.

Sleep, crop and herd. Sleep, darkling thorpe and croft.
　　Safe from the weather.
He, whom we convoy to his grave aloft,
　　Singing together,
He was a man born with thy face and throat,
　　Lyric Apollo !
Long he lived nameless : how should spring take note
　　Winter would follow ?
Till lo, the little touch, and youth was gone.
　　Cramped and diminished,
Moaned he, " New measures, other feet anon.
　　My dance is finished " ?
No, that's the world's way (keep the mountain-side,
　　Make for the city) :
He knew the signal, and stepped on with pride
　　Over men's pity ;
Left play for work, and grappled with the world
　　Bent on escaping :
" What's in the scroll ", quoth he, " thou keepest
　　　furled ?
　　Show me their shaping,
Theirs who most studied man, the bard and sage,—
　　Give."   So, he gowned him,
Straight got by heart that book to its last page :
　　Learned, we found him.
Yea, but we found him bald too, eyes like lead,
　　Accents uncertain ;
" Time to taste life ", another would have said,

" Up with the curtain."
This man said rather, " Actual life comes next ?
    Patience a moment.
Grant I have mastered learning's crabbed text,
    Still there's the comment.
Let me know all.   Prate not of most or least,
    Painful or easy ;
Even to the crumbs I'd fain eat up the feast,
    Ay, nor feel queasy."
Oh, such a life as he resolved to live,
    When he had learned it,
When he had gathered all books had to give :
    Sooner, he spurned it.
Image the whole, then execute the parts,
    Fancy the fabric
Quite, ere you build, ere steel strike fire from quartz,
    Ere mortar dab brick.

(Here's the town-gate reached : there's the market-
    place
    Gaping before us.)
Yea, this in him was the peculiar grace
    (Hearten our chorus.)
That before living he'd learn how to live—
    No end to learning :
Earn the means first—God surely will contrive
    Use for our earning.
Others mistrust and say, " But time escapes :
    Live now or never."
He said, " What's time ?   Leave Now for dogs and
    apes ;

Man has For Ever."
Back to his book then : deeper drooped his head ;
   Calculus racked him ;
Leaden before, his eyes grew dross of lead ;
   Tussis attacked him.
" Now, master, take a little rest."   Not he !
   (Caution redoubled,
Step two abreast, the way winds narrowly.)
   Not a whit troubled,
Back to his studies, fresher than at first,
   Fierce as a dragon
He, soul-hydroptic with a sacred thirst,
   Sucked at the flagon.
Oh, if we draw a circle premature,
   Heedless of far gain,
Greedy for quick returns of profit, sure
   Bad is our bargain.
Was it not great ?   Did not he throw on God
   (He loves the burthen)
God's task to make the heavenly period
   Perfect the earthen ?
Did not he magnify the mind, show clear
   Just what it all meant ?
He would not discount life, as fools do here,
   Paid by instalment.
He ventured neck or nothing—heaven's success
   Found, or earth's failure :
" Wilt thou trust death or not ? "   He answered " Yes :
   Hence with life's pale lure ! "
That low man seeks a little thing to do,
   Sees it and does it :

This high man, with a great thing to pursue,
    Dies ere he knows it.
That low man goes on adding one to one,
    His hundred's soon hit :
This high man, aiming at a million,
    Misses a unit.
That, has the world here—should he need the next,
    Let the world mind him :
This, throws himself on God, and unperplexed
    Seeking shall find Him.
So, with the throttling hands of death at strife,
    Ground he at grammar ;
Still, through the rattle, parts of speech were rife :
    While he could stammer
He settled *Hoti's* business—let it be—
    Properly based *Oun*,
Gave us the doctrine of the enclitic *De*,
    Dead from the waist down.
Well, here's the platform, here's the proper place :
    Hail to your purlieus,
All ye high-fliers of the feathered race,
    Swallows and curlews !
Here's the top peak ; the multitude below
    Live, for they can, there :
This man decided not to Live but Know—
    Bury this man there ?
Here—here's his place, where meteors shoot, clouds
    form,
    Lightnings are loosened,
Stars come and go.   Let joy break with the storm,
    Peace let the dew send.

Lofty designs must close in like effects :
  Loftily lying,
Leave him—still loftier than the world suspects,
  Living and dying.

 A Grammarian's Funeral is perhaps the most difficult of
the poems included in this selection, but not only is it a
much admired piece of verse, a quarry for quotations, but
also very typical of its author in subject, thought, and
technique. It is one of the best of Browning's studies of
the Renaissance. In this " Revival of Learning " the pursuit of knowledge, especially the knowledge to be won
from Greece and Rome, was carried on with a hungry
passion which in our degenerate days we can admire rather
than emulate. Browning's originality, and his delight in
setting himself a hard task, are shown by his choosing as
his hero, as his example of this sacred thirst for learning,
a Grammarian, and a dry-as-dust Grammarian, who has
laboured after explaining the functions of ancient Greek
adverbs and particles. But his disciples have no doubt of
the greatness of this man who " decided not to Live but
Know ", and they honour him by carrying his body to its
burial-place in " the appropriate country ", the top of a
high mountain, symbolic at once of his infinite search for
knowledge and of his superiority to the common herd.
The lurching metre, alternating long breaths and gasps,
and perhaps also the sudden jolts in expression—" he
settled *Hoti's* business "—are a clever reflection of the
stumbling journey up the rough mountain-side.
 Some of Browning's favourite ideas are expressed in the
poem. One, already met with in *The Patriot*, is that to
devote oneself to a high ideal unattainable in this life is
better than to succeed in a lower aim.

  That low man goes on adding one to one,
   His hundred's soon hit :
  This high man, aiming at a million,
   Misses a unit.

G

A corollary of this idea is an unquestioning belief in personal immortality. It is in the life to come that a noble failure here will be crowned with success.

He said, " What's time ?   Leave Now for dogs and apes ;
      Man has For Ever."

The poem has three paragraphs of unequal length. The first describes how the Grammarian's disciples, " singing together ", carry his body in triumph up the mountain. This is metaphorically said to be " citied to the top, crowded with culture ". It is symbolic of the higher reaches of thought, and towers above " the unlettered plain ", representative of the ignorance of the common multitude.   On the other hand, the citadel " circling its summit " is a real citadel, a fortified little town through whose market-place (see the opening lines of the third paragraph) the procession eventually marches.

The second paragraph, with its rapid changes of metaphor, requires careful reading.   The Grammarian was born with the beauty of feature represented in the statues of Apollo, the Greek god of lyric poetry. He gained no fame in his youth ; but when this had passed he did not complain mournfully that " my dance is finished ", that the worth-whileness of life was over. On the contrary, he devoted himself to learning, to interpreting the work, so far partly a sealed book, of the great Classical poets and philosophers. Scholars now gathered round him, to find him an old man, bald, stammering, leaden-eyed. Another might have said, " Now that I am famous it is time to enjoy life." But the Grammarian would not rest content ; he had mastered the crabbed text of learning, but there was still the commentary—a metaphor taken from medieval books where text and commentary were on the same page, or on opposite pages. He was eager to know all that he could know ; he had grasped the meaning of the whole, but had still to study the parts, like an architect who plans the whole fabric before any portion of it is executed,

> Ere mortar dab brick,

—certainly one of the cleverest of Browning's rhymes.

The third paragraph, which contains the main ideas of the poem, has fewer difficulties. Back to his books, the Grammarian was attacked by disease, stone in the kidneys (*calculus*) and bronchitis (*tussis*). But he still aimed at the whole of knowledge, and would not be satisfied with mere instalments. Even with death approaching " ground he at grammar ", and discovered the functions of the Greek conjunction *hoti* (" that "), the Greek adverb *oun* (" therefore "), and of the enclitic *de*. The poem ends with the arrival of the procession at the top of the mountain, where the scholars bury their master, leaving him

> Still loftier than the world suspects,
> Living and dying.

In reading the poem care should be taken to observe marks of interrogation, which are sometimes the only means of distinguishing between a rhetorical question and a statement or command.

Thorpes : hamlets. *Sepulture :* burial-place. *'Ware the beholders :* let the onlookers be aware of it. *Darkling :* in the dark (adverb used as adjective). *Soul-hydroptic :* with a soul eager to drink. *The enclitic de :* an enclitic is an unemphatic particle added to a preceding word ; Greek *de* as an enclitic had the sense of " towards ". *Purlieus :* haunts.

15. THE BISHOP ORDERS HIS TOMB AT SAINT PRAXED'S CHURCH

VANITY, saith the preacher, vanity !
Draw round my bed : is Anselm keeping back ?
Nephews—sons mine . . . ah God, I know not. Well—
She, men would have to be your mother once,
Old Gandolf envied me, so fair she was.
What's done is done, and she is dead beside,
Dead long ago, and I am Bishop since,
And as she died so must we die ourselves,
And thence ye may perceive the world's a dream.
Life, how and what is it ?   As here I lie
In this state-chamber, dying by degrees,
Hours and long hours in the dead night, I ask
" Do I live, am I dead ? "   Peace, peace seems all.
Saint Praxed's ever was the church for peace ;
And so, about this tomb of mine.   I fought
With tooth and nail to save my niche, ye know :
Old Gandolf cozened me, despite my care ;
Shrewd was that snatch from out the corner South
He graced his carrion with, God curse the same !
Yet still my niche is not so cramped but thence
One sees the pulpit o' the epistle-side,
And somewhat of the choir, those silent seats,
And up into the aery dome where live
The angels, and a sunbeam's sure to lurk :
And I shall fill my slab of basalt there,
And 'neath my tabernacle take my rest,
With those nine columns round me, two and two,

The odd one at my feet where Anselm stands :
Peach-blossom marble all, the rare, the ripe
As fresh-poured red wine of a mighty pulse.
—Old Gandolf with his paltry onion-stone,
Put me where I may look at him.   True peach,
Rosy and flawless : how I earned the prize !
Draw close : that conflagration of my church—
What then ?   So much was saved if aught were missed.
My sons, ye would not be my death ?   Go dig
The white-grape vineyard where the oil-press stood,
Drop water gently till the surface sink,
And if ye find—ah God, I know not, I—
Bedded in store of rotten fig-leaves soft,
And corded up in a tight olive-frail,
Some lump, ah God, of lapis lazuli,
Big as a Jew's head cut off at the nape,
Blue as a vein o'er the Madonna's breast—
Sons, all have I bequeathed you, villas, all,
That brave Frascati villa with its bath—
So, let the blue lump poise between my knees,
Like God the Father's globe on both his hands
Ye worship in the Jesu Church so gay,
For Gandolf shall not choose but see and burst.
Swift as a weaver's shuttle fleet our years :
Man goeth to the grave, and where is he ?
Did I say basalt for my slab, sons ?   Black—
'Twas ever antique-black I meant.   How else
Shall ye contrast my frieze to come beneath ?
The bas-relief in bronze ye promised me,
Those Pans and Nymphs ye wot of, and perchance
Some tripod, thyrsus, with a vase or so,

The Saviour at his sermon on the mount,
Saint Praxed in a glory, and one Pan
Ready to twitch the Nymph's last garment off,
And Moses with the tables—but I know
Ye mark me not.   What do they whisper thee,
Child of my bowels, Anselm ?   Ah, ye hope
To revel down my villas while I gasp
Bricked o'er with beggar's mouldy travertine
Which Gandolf from his tomb-top chuckles at.
Nay, boys, ye love me—all of jasper, then ;
'Tis jasper ye stand pledged to, lest I grieve.
My bath must needs be left behind, alas !
One block, pure green as a pistachio nut—
There's plenty jasper somewhere in the world :
And have I not Saint Praxed's ear to pray
Horses for ye, and brown Greek manuscripts,
And mistresses with great smooth marbly limbs ?
—That's if ye carve my epitaph aright,
Choice Latin, picked phrase, Tully's every word,
No gaudy ware like Gandolf's second line—
Tully, my masters ?   Ulpian serves his need.
And then how I shall lie through centuries,
And hear the blessed mutter of the mass,
And see God made and eaten all day long,
And feel the steady candle-flame, and taste
Good strong thick stupefying incense-smoke !
For, as I lie here, hours of the dead night,
Dying in state and by such slow degrees,
I fold my arms as if they clasped a crook,
And stretch my feet forth straight as stone can point,
And let the bed-clothes, for a mortcloth, drop

Into great laps and folds of sculptor's work :
And, as yon tapers dwindle, and strange thoughts
Grow, with a certain humming in my ears,
About the life before I lived this life,
And this life too, popes, cardinals, and priests,
Saint Praxed at his sermon on the mount,
Your tall pale mother with her talking eyes,
And new-found agate urns as fresh as day,
And marble's language, Latin pure, discreet—
Aha, ELUCESCEBAT quoth our friend ?
No Tully, said I, Ulpian at the best.
Evil and brief hath been my pilgrimage—
All lapis, all, sons.   Else I give the Pope
My villas.   Will ye ever eat my heart ?
Ever your eyes were as a lizard's quick,
They glitter like your mother's for my soul,
Or ye would heighten my impoverished frieze,
Piece out its starved design, and fill my vase
With grapes, and add a vizor and a Term,
And to the tripod ye would tie a lynx
That in his struggle throws the thyrsus down,
To comfort me on my entablature
Whereon I am to lie till I must ask
" Do I live, am I dead ? "   There, leave me, there !
For ye have stabbed me with ingratitude
To death—ye wish it—God, ye wish it !   Stone—
Gritstone, a-crumble !   Clammy squares which sweat
As if the corpse they keep were oozing through,
And no more lapis to delight the world !
Well, go !   I bless ye.   Fewer tapers there,
But in a row : and, going, turn your backs,

Ay, like departing altar-ministrants,
And leave me in my church, the church for peace,
That I may watch at leisure if he leers—
Old Gandolf, at me, from his onion-stone,
As still he envied me, so fair she was.

Character-portrayal by means of monologue has perhaps never been done with greater vividness than in this poem. At the same time it gives us a view of the Italian Renaissance in its decadence. The scene is Rome in the sixteenth century. The old Bishop, his mind wandering somewhat as he lies slowly dying, so that sometimes he is not quite sure whether he is alive or dead, and tends to confuse himself and his effigy, yet earnestly adjuring his sons to build him a tomb which will be a miracle of ornate sculpture and an amazing mixture of Pagan and Christian themes, and fully disclosing in his monologue his passion for art, beauty, and Ciceronian Latin, his memories of his sons' tall pale mother, his malicious dislike of his rival, old Gandolf, his petulant doubts of his sons' willingness to carry out his wishes, and a certain pathetic craving for peace, all this interspersed with unctuous moralisings on the vanity of human life, is one of the most rounded humorous characters that we have in English literature. The tolerance of Browning's presentation of him makes one finish the poem with a feeling of sympathy for the worldly old reprobate, and with the hope that his sons will at least build him a monument which will give old Gandolf, on his paltry onion-stone, no justification for a chuckle.

St. Praxed's Church is in Rome, and its interior is richly decorated. Saint Praxed was a virgin saint said to be the daughter of a Roman centurion of the first century after Christ. In the first line " the preacher " is Ecclesiastes. The natural sons of a medieval cleric were euphemistically termed his nephews. The epistle-side of the church is the south side; the New Testament Epistles were read from the right of the altar. Frascati, which used to contain opulent villas, is twelve miles south-east of Rome. The Bishop wishes his effigy to lie on a slab of black basalt, beneath which should be a frieze or bas-relief, a horizontal band of bronze with sculptured decoration. Tully is Cicero, a model of Classical Latin; Ulpian is Ulpianus Domitius, a late Roman legal writer (died A.D. 228), whose Latin was not considered to be pure. "Saint Praxed at his sermon on the mount" is a sign of the dying Bishop's enfeebled wits; he is confusing Saint Praxed and Christ.

Olive-frail: a rush basket for holding olives. *Lapis lazuli, lapis*: a blue semi-precious stone. *Thyrsus*: a wreathed staff. *Travertine* (also found in *Pictor Ignotus*): a kind of lime-stone. *Mort-cloth*: a winding-sheet. *Term*: a bust ending in a square stone pillar, an ancient boundary mark.

16. PICTOR IGNOTUS

I COULD have painted pictures like that youth's
    Ye praise so. How my soul springs up ! No bar
Stayed me—ah, thought which saddens while it
    soothes !—
  —Never did fate forbid me, star by star,
To outburst on your night with all my gift
    Of fires from God ; nor would my flesh have shrunk
From seconding my soul, with eyes uplift
    And wide to heaven, or, straight like thunder, sunk
To the centre, of an instant ; or around
    Turned calmly and inquisitive, to scan
The licence and the limit, space and bound,
    Allowed to truth made visible in man :
And, like that youth ye praise so, all I saw,
    Over the canvas could my hand have flung,
Each face obedient to its passion's law,
    Each passion clear proclaimed without a tongue ;
Whether Hope rose at once in all the blood,
    A-tiptoe for the blessing of embrace,
Or Rapture drooped the eyes, as when her brood
    Pull down the nesting dove's heart to its place ;
Or Confidence lit swift the forehead up,
    And locked the mouth fast, like a castle braved—
O human faces, hath it spilt, my cup ?
    What did ye give me that I have not saved?
Nor will I say I have not dreamed (how well !)
    Of going—I, in each new picture—forth,
As, making new hearts beat and bosoms swell,

To Pope or Kaiser, East, West, South, or North,
Bound for the calmly satisfied great State,
   Or glad aspiring little burgh, it went,
Flowers cast upon the car which bore the freight,
   Through old streets named afresh from the event,
Till it reached home, where learned age should greet
   My face, and youth, the star not yet distinct
Above his hair, lie learning at my feet.
   O, thus to live, I and my picture, linked
With love about, and praise, till life should end,
   And then not go to heaven, but linger here,
Here on my earth, earth's every man my friend—
   The thought grew frightful, 'twas so wildly
      dear !
But a voice changed it.　Glimpses of such sights
   Have scared me, like the revels through a door
Of some strange house of idols at its rites ;
   This world seemed not the world it was before.
Mixed with my loving trusting ones, there trooped—
   Who summoned those cold faces that begun
To press on me and judge me ?　Though I stooped
   Shrinking, as from the soldiery a nun,
They drew me forth, and spite of me—enough !
   These buy and sell our pictures, take and give,
Count them for garniture and household-stuff,
   And where they live needs must our pictures
      live
And see their faces, listen to their prate,
   Partakers of their daily pettiness,
Discussed of—" This I love, or this I hate,
   This likes me more, and this affects me less."

Wherefore I chose my portion.   If at whiles
　My heart sinks, as monotonous I paint
These endless cloisters and eternal aisles
　With the same series, Virgin, Babe, and Saint,
With the same cold calm beautiful regard—
　At least no merchant traffics in my heart;
The sanctuary's gloom at least shall ward
　Vain tongues from where my pictures stand apart.
Only prayer breaks the silence of the shrine
　While, blackening in the daily candle-smoke,
They moulder on the damp wall's travertine,
　'Mid echoes the light footstep never woke.
So, die my pictures ! surely, gently die !
O youth, men praise so, holds their praise its
　　worth ?
　Blown harshly, keeps the trump its golden cry ?
Tastes sweet the water with such specks of earth ?

Pictor Ignotus is a sympathetic study of a timid sensitive
soul, who has wishful dreams of the fame that would be his
if he painted pictures " like that youth's ye praise so ", but
shrinks fearfully away from the contact with a critical and
mercenary world that he and his pictures would then have
to undergo.   The scene of the monologue is Florence in
the sixteenth century.   In that heyday of Italian art a great
painting was looked upon as a triumph of human endeavour,
and might be carried in joyful procession to its destined
home " through old streets named afresh from the event ".
Browning had probably in mind the Borgo Allegri in
Florence, so named after a famous painting of the Madonna
had been borne along it.
　The title means " Painter Unknown ".   " Sunk to the
centre ", that is, " sank back from heaven to earth ", the
centre of the universe according to medieval ideas.   The

two lines beginning " O human faces " are difficult; the meaning seems to be, " The cup of my memory has been filled to overflowing with human faces, and I have preserved in my mind all the various expressions that I have seen in these.'

17. A TOCCATA OF GALUPPI'S

Oh Galuppi, Baldassaro, this is very sad to find :
I can hardly misconceive you ; it would prove me deaf
and blind ;
But although I take your meaning, 'tis with such a
heavy mind.

Here you come with your old music, and here's all the
good it brings.
What, they lived once thus at Venice where the
merchants were the kings,
Where Saint Mark's is, where the Doges used to wed
the sea with rings ?

Ay, because the sea's the street there ; and 'tis arched
by . . . what you call
Shylock's bridge with houses on it, where they kept
the carnival :
I was never out of England—it's as if I saw it all.

Did young people take their pleasure when the sea
was warm in May ?
Balls and masks begun at midnight, burning ever to
mid-day,
When they made up fresh adventures for the morrow,
do you say ?

Was a lady such a lady, cheeks so round and lips so red,
On her neck the small face buoyant, like a bell-flower
on its bed,

O'er the breast's superb abundance where a man
  might base his head ?

Well, and it was graceful of them—they'd break talk
  off and afford
—She, to bite her mask's black velvet, he, to finger
  on his sword,
While you sat and played Toccatas, stately at the
  clavichord.

What ? Those lesser thirds so plaintive, sixths
  diminished, sigh on sigh,
Told them something ? Those suspensions, those
  solutions—" Must we die ? "
Those commiserating sevenths—" Life might last.
  We can but try."

" Were you happy ? "—" Yes."—" And are you still
  as happy ? "—" Yes.   And you ? "
" Then, more kisses ! "—" Did I stop them, when a
  million seemed so few ? "
Hark, the dominant's persistence till it must be
  answered to !

So, an octave struck the answer. Oh, they praised
  you, I dare say.
" Brave Galuppi ! That was music ! Good alike at
  grave and gay !
I can always leave off talking when I hear a master
  play."

Then they left you for their pleasure : till in due time,
one by one,
Some with lives that came to nothing, some with
deeds as well undone,
Death stepped tacitly and took them where they never
see the sun.

But when I sit down to reason, think to take my stand
nor swerve,
While I triumph o'er a secret wrung from nature's
close reserve,
In you come with your cold music till I creep through
every nerve.

Yes, you, like a ghostly cricket, creaking where a
house was burned :
" Dust and ashes, dead and done with, Venice spent
what Venice earned.
The soul, doubtless, is immortal—where a soul can be
discerned.

Yours, for instance : you know physics, something of
geology,
Mathematics are your pastime ; souls shall rise in their
degree ;
Butterflies may dread extinction, you'll not die, it
cannot be !

As for Venice and her people, merely born to bloom
and drop,

Here on earth they bore their fruitage, mirth and folly
     were the crop :
What of soul was left, I wonder, when the kissing had
     to stop ?

Dust and ashes ! " So you creak it, and I want the
     heart to scold.
Dear dead women, with such hair, too—what's become
     of all the gold
Used to hang and brush their bosoms ? I feel chilly
     and grown old.

Browning was taught music in his youth, and was a
competent performer with a keen interest in the art. *A
Toccata of Galuppi's* is the earliest of several poems whose
theme is music and the emotions or ideas that it expresses
or suggests. Baldassare Galuppi was an Italian composer
of the eighteenth century, whose principal works were
light operas, and who in 1768 became organist in St. Mark's
Cathedral in Venice. A toccata or " touch-piece " is a
preliminary flourish or overture ; as a rule it plays lightly
and superficially with the theme of the music that follows,
so that the introduction of solemn or melancholy chords
into it will quite naturally suggest the contrast between
the gaiety of life and the annihilation of death. Browning,
like Kipling, is apt to display his knowledge of technical
terms, and those in stanzas 7 and 8, " lesser thirds ",
" the dominant ", etc., are incomprehensible to anyone
without a musical training. But all that one need grasp is
the general idea, that while the toccata mirrors the joy of
life and youth and love, and suggests the lovers' talk in
stanza 8, it nevertheless, by more plaintive and lingering
chords, also conveys the warning of " dust and ashes ".
     The poem is a dramatic lyric, spoken by a man with
scientific knowledge and interests, who wrings secrets

H

"from nature's close reserve" (stanzas 11 and 13). Listening to the toccata he can, although he has never been out of England, imagine Venice of the eighteenth century and its brilliant but transient gaiety. He feels that the music brings the same warning message to himself. The Venetian butterflies had perhaps no souls worthy of survival into a future life, but can even a learned scientist be sure that his own soul will be ranked of higher value?

Notwithstanding its occasional difficulties, *A Toccata of Galuppi's* is one of Browning's most pleasing lyrics, and the last two stanzas are among the most musical that he ever wrote.

Venice, built on small islands on the Adriatic Sea, with canals instead of streets, was in medieval and early modern times a city of merchant princes and a great naval power. Its chief magistrate, the Doge, used every year to throw a ring into the Adriatic as a symbol of the union between the city and the sea. The supposed house of Shylock is still shown near the Rialto Bridge. A clavichord is a predecessor of the piano.

18. HOME THOUGHTS, FROM ABROAD

OH, to be in England
Now that April's there,
And whoever wakes in England
Sees, some morning, unaware,
That the lowest boughs and the brushwood sheaf
Round the elm-tree bole are in tiny leaf,
While the chaffinch sings on the orchard bough
In England—now !

And after April, when May follows,
And the whitethroat builds, and all the swallows !
Hark, where my blossomed pear-tree in the hedge
Leans to the field and scatters on the clover
Blossoms and dewdrops, at the bent spray's edge—
That's the wise thrush ; he sings each song twice over,
Lest you should think he never could recapture
The first fine careless rapture,
And though the fields look rough with hoary dew
All will be gay when noontide wakes anew
The buttercups, the little children's dower
—Far brighter than this gaudy melon-flower.

The poem expresses the mood of home-sickness which
comes upon an Englishman abroad at the thought of the
freshness of an English spring in April and May. In a
series of rapid flashes Browning shows us typically English
sights and sounds ; and his description of the repeated lilt
of the thrush's song is one of the most memorable things
in his poetry.

The " elm-tree bole " is the trunk of the elm.

19. DE GUSTIBUS—

Your ghost will walk, you lover of trees,
        (If our loves remain)
        In an English lane,
By a cornfield-side a-flutter with poppies.
Hark, those two in the hazel coppice—
A boy and a girl, if the good fates please,
        Making love, say—
        The happier they !
Draw yourself up from the light of the moon,
And let them pass, as they will too soon,
        With the bean-flowers' boon,
        And the blackbird's tune,
        And May, and June.

What I love best in all the world
Is a castle, precipice-encurled,
In a gash of the wind-grieved Apennine :
Or look for me, old fellow of mine,
(If I get my head from out the mouth
O' the grave, and loose my spirit's bands,
And come again to the land of lands)
In a sea-side house to the farther South,
Where the baked cicala dies of drouth,
And one sharp tree—'tis a cypress—stands,
By the many hundred years red-rusted,
Rough iron-spiked, ripe-fruit-o'ercrusted,
My sentinel to guard the sands
To the water's edge.   For, what expands

Before the house, but the great opaque
Blue breadth of sea without a break ?
While, in the house, for ever crumbles
Some fragment of the frescoed walls
From blisters where a scorpion sprawls.
A girl bare-footed brings, and tumbles
Down on the pavement, green-flesh melons,
And says there's news to-day—the king
Was shot at, touched in the liver-wing,
Goes with his Bourbon arm in a sling :
—She hopes they have not caught the felons.
Italy, my Italy !
Queen Mary's saying serves for me—
    (When fortune's malice
    Lost her Calais)
Open my heart and you will see
Graved inside of it, " Italy ".
Such lovers old are I and she :
So it always was, so shall ever be.

" De Gustibus—" is from the Latin proverb, *De gustibus
non est disputandum*, " there's no disputing about tastes ".
A personal lyric, it expresses the poet's love for his adopted
country, Italy, " the land of lands ". Most of it consists
of two masterly pieces of scene-painting, in which the
happy quietude of an English country lane is contrasted
with the brilliant grotesqueness of the baked sea-coast in
southern Italy ; and it should be observed that Browning
brings a human interest into both.

The second line is a condensed way of saying, " If after
death we love what we have loved during life ". The
cicala or cicada is a large beetle noted for its loud shrill
cry. About 1850, when the poem was written, the

south of Italy was the kingdom of Naples, ruled by the unpopular Ferdinand the Second, belonging to the Bourbon family, whom his subjects took delight in shooting at. The liver-wing is the right wing of a cooked fowl, since the liver is usually tucked under it ; hence, by a colloquial metaphor, the right arm. Queen Mary, the elder sister of Queen Elizabeth, reigned from 1553 to 1558. When the French captured Calais, the last English possession in France, she is said to have exclaimed that when she died Calais would be found written on her heart.

20. UP AT A VILLA—DOWN IN THE CITY

(AS DISTINGUISHED BY AN ITALIAN PERSON
OF QUALITY)

HAD I but plenty of money, money enough and to
    spare,
The house for me, no doubt, were a house in the city
    square ;
Ah, such a life, such a life, as one leads at the window
    there !

Something to see, by Bacchus, something to hear, at
    least ;
There, the whole day long, one's life is a perfect feast,
While up at a villa one lives, I maintain it, no more
    than a beast.

Well, now, look at our villa, stuck like the horn of a bull
Just on a mountain-edge as bare as the creature's skull,
Save a mere shag of a bush with hardly a leaf to pull.
I scratch my own, sometimes, to see if the hair's turned
    wool.

But the city, oh the city ! The square with the
    houses ! Why,
They are stone-faced, white as a curd, there's some-
    thing to take the eye,
Houses in four straight lines, not a single front awry ;
You watch who crosses and gossips, who saunters,
    who hurries by ;

Green blinds, as a matter of course, to draw when the
  sun gets high ;
And the shops with fanciful signs which are painted
  properly.

What of a villa ? Though winter be over in March by
  rights,
'Tis May perhaps ere the snow shall have withered
  well off the heights :
You've the brown ploughed land before, where the
  oxen steam and wheeze,
And the hills over-smoked behind by the faint grey
  olive-trees.

Is it better in May, I ask you ? You've summer all at
  once ;
In a day he leaps complete with a few strong April suns.
'Mid the sharp short emerald wheat, scarce risen three
  fingers well,
The wild tulip, at end of its tube, blows out its great
  red bell
Like a thin clear bubble of blood, for the children to
  pick and sell.

Is it ever hot in the square ? There's a fountain to
  spout and splash ;
In the shade it sings and springs ; in the shine such
  foam-bows flash
On the horses with curling fish-tails, that prance and
  paddle and pash

Round the lady atop in her conch fifty gazers do not
    abash,
Though all that she wears is some weeds round her
    waist in a sort of sash.

All the year long at the villa, nothing to see though
    you linger,
Except yon cypress that points like death's lean lifted
    forefinger.
Some think fireflies pretty, when they mix i' the corn
    and mingle,
Or thrid the stinking hemp till the stalks of it seem
    a-tingle.
Late August or early September, the stunning cicala
    is shrill,
And the bees keep their tiresome whine round the
    resinous firs on the hill.
Enough of the seasons—I spare you the months of
    the fever and chill.

Ere you open your eyes in the city, the blessed church-
    bells begin :
No sooner the bells leave off than the diligence rattles
    in ;
You get the pick of the news, and it costs you never
    a pin.
By-and-by there's the travelling doctor gives pills, lets
    blood, draws teeth ;
Or the Pulcinello-trumpet breaks up the market
    beneath.

At the post-office such a scene-picture—the new play,
    piping hot,
And a notice how, only this morning, three liberal
    thieves were shot.
Above it, behold the Archbishop's most fatherly of
    rebukes,
And beneath, with his crown and his lion, some little
    new law of the Duke's ;
Or a sonnet with flowery marge, to the Reverend Don
    So-and-so
Who is Dante, Boccaccio, Petrarca, Saint Jerome, and
    Cicero,
" And moreover " (the sonnet goes rhyming) " the
    skirts of Saint Paul has reached,
Having preached us those six Lent-lectures more
    unctuous than ever he preached."
Noon strikes—here sweeps the procession, our Lady
    borne smiling and smart
With a pink gauze gown all spangles, and seven
    swords stuck in her heart.
Bang-whang-whang goes the drum, *tootle-te-tootle* the
    fife ;
No keeping one's haunches still : it's the greatest
    pleasure in life.

But bless you, it's dear, it's dear. Fowls, wine, at
    double the rate !
They have clapped a new tax upon salt, and what oil
    pays passing the gate
It's a horror to think of. And so, the villa for me,
    not the city ;

Beggars can scarcely be choosers, but still—ah, the pity, the pity !

Look, two and two go the priests, then the monks with cowls and sandals,

And the penitents dressed in white shirts, a-holding the yellow candles ;

One, he carries a flag up straight, and another a cross with handles,

And the Duke's guard brings up the rear, for the better prevention of scandals ;

Bang-whang-whang goes the drum, *tootle-te-tootle* the fife.

Oh, a day in the city-square, there is no such pleasure in life !

The poem shows Browning's lively observation both of the Italian countryside, with its olive groves like grey smoke on the hills, and of the bustle, excitement and showy, shabby pageantry of Italian city life. It is placed in the mouth of a " person of quality ", who is bored with vegetating in his country villa, but cannot afford to carry out his dearest wish and live in the central square of the town.

The horses with curling fish-tails, and the lady in her conch or large shell, are the statuary of the city fountain. The Pulcinello-trumpet is the trumpet announcing a Punch-and-Judy show. To the person of quality revolutionaries are " liberal thieves ". The " flowery marge " of the sonnet is the floral decoration round the page on which it is written or printed. The seven swords stuck in Our Lady's heart symbolise the seven sorrows of the Blessed Virgin—an enumeration that goes back to medieval times. " What oil pays passing the gate " refers to the *octroi* or dues levied upon provisions entering the city.

Shag : untidy tangle. *Thrid :* thread. *Diligence :* stage-coach.

21. TIME'S REVENGES

I'VE a Friend, over the sea ;
I like him, but he loves me.
It all grew out of the books I write ;
They find such favour in his sight
That he slaughters you with savage looks
Because you don't admire my books.
He does himself though, and if some vein
Were to snap to-night in this heavy brain,
To-morrow month, if I lived to try,
Round should I just turn quietly,
Or out of the bed-clothes stretch my hand
Till I found him, come from his foreign land
To be my nurse in this poor place,
And make my broth and wash my face
And light my fire and, all the while,
Bear with his old good-humoured smile
That I told him, " Better have kept away
Than come and kill me, night and day,
With, worse than fever throbs and shoots,
The creaking of his clumsy boots."
I am as sure that this he would do
As that Saint Paul's is striking two.
And I think I rather—woe is me !—
Yes, rather would see him than not see,
If lifting a hand could seat him there
Before me in the empty chair
To-night, when my head aches indeed,
And I can neither think nor read,

Nor make these purple fingers hold
The pen ; this garret's freezing cold.

And I've a Lady—there he wakes,
The laughing fiend and prince of snakes
Within me, at her name, to pray
Fate send some creature in the way
Of my love for her, to be down-torn,
Upthrust and outward-borne,
So I might prove myself that sea
Of passion which I needs must be.
Call my thoughts false and my fancies quaint,
And my style infirm and its figures faint,
All the critics say, and more blame yet,
And not one angry word you get :
But, please you, wonder I would put
My cheek beneath that lady's foot
Rather than trample under mine
The laurels of the Florentine,
And you shall see how the devil spends
A fire God gave for other ends.
I tell you, I stride up and down
This garret, crowned with love's best crown,
And feasted with love's perfect feast,
To think I kill for her, at least,
Body and soul and peace and fame,
Alike youth's end and manhood's aim.
—So is my spirit, as flesh with sin,
Filled full, eaten out and in
With the face of her, the eyes of her,
The lips, the little chin, the stir

Of shadow round her mouth ; and she—
I'll tell you—calmly would decree
That I should roast at a slow fire,
If that would compass her desire
And make her one whom they invite
To the famous ball to-morrow night.

There may be heaven ; there must be hell ;
Meantime, there is our earth here—well !

The speaker, a poor author in a London garret, has a
friend in another land who admires and loves him, and
would do anything for him ; but all that he can say in
return for this devotion is that he " would rather see him
than not see ". On the other hand the lady whom he
passionately adores, and for whom he has sacrificed

Body and soul and peace and fame,
Alike youth's end and manhood's aim,

cares nothing at all for him. " And thus ", says the Clown
at the end of Shakespeare's *Twelfth Night*, " the whirlegigge
of time brings in his revenges."

The poem is a fine example of Browning's power of
giving effective expression to a consuming passion by
means of language that is simple and often colloquial.

Figures in *my figures faint* means figures of speech. *The
Florentine* is the great Italian poet Dante. The general
meaning of the last two lines is that possibly heaven, and
certainly hell, are to be found in life in this world.

22. YOUTH AND ART

It once might have been, once only :
  We lodged in a street together,
You, a sparrow on the house-top lonely,
  I, a lone she-bird of his feather.

Your trade was with sticks and clay,
  You thumbed, thrust, patted and polished,
Then laughed " They will see some day
  Smith made, and Gibson demolished ".

My business was song, song, song ;
  I chirped, cheeped, trilled and twittered,
" Kate Brown's on the boards ere long,
  And Grisi's existence embittered".

I earned no more by a warble
  Than you by a sketch in plaster;
You wanted a piece of marble,
  I needed a music-master.

We studied hard in our styles,
  Chipped each at a crust like Hindoos,
For air looked out on the tiles,
  For fun watched each other's windows.

You lounged, like a boy of the South,
  Cap and blouse—nay, a bit of beard too ;
Or you got it, rubbing your mouth
  With fingers the clay adhered to.

And I—soon managed to find
    Weak points in the flower-fence facing,
Was forced to put up a blind
    And be safe in my corset-lacing.

No harm ! It was not my fault
    If you never turned your eye's tail up
As I shook upon E *in alt*,
    Or ran the chromatic scale up :

For spring bade the sparrows pair,
    And the boys and girls gave guesses,
And stalls in our street looked rare
    With bulrush and watercresses.

Why did not you pinch a flower
    In a pellet of clay and fling it ?
Why did not I put a power
    Of thanks in a look, or sing it ?

I did look, sharp as a lynx,
    (And yet the memory rankles)
When models arrived, some minx
    Tripped upstairs, she and her ankles.

But I think I gave you as good :
    " That foreign fellow—who can know
How she pays, in a playful mood,
    For his tuning her that piano ? "

Could you say so, and never say
    " Suppose we join hands and fortunes,

And I fetch her from over the way,
  Her, piano, and long tunes and short tunes " ?

No, no : You would not be rash,
  Nor I rasher and something over ;
You've to settle yet Gibson's hash,
  And Grisi yet lives in clover.

But you meet the Prince at the Board,
  I'm queen myself at *bals-paré*,
I've married a rich old lord,
  And you're dubbed knight and an R.A.

Each life unfulfilled, you see ;
  It hangs still, patchy and scrappy :
We have not sighed deep, laughed free,
  Starved, feasted, despaired—been happy.

And nobody calls you a dunce,
  And people suppose me clever :
This could but have happened once,
  And we missed it, lost it for ever.

Youth and Art is the most attractive of several poems by Browning on the theme of the supreme importance of love for the fulfilment of life. The speaker, the singer Kate Brown, and the sculptor Smith were, when young, poor artists living and working in garrets at opposite sides of the street, presumably in Rome. They had the opportunity of love, but prudence and ambition prevailed ; and now they have gained worldly success in their separate arts. But their lives remain incomplete, and they have missed

I

the chance of perfect happiness. There is no tragic feeling in the poem ; it expresses a rueful regret over what might have been. The metaphor of the two sparrows on the house-tops with which it begins finds an echo in the almost chirpy trill of the style and verse.

John Gibson was a successful English sculptor, and Giulia Grisi a famous Italian operatic singer, of the middle of the nineteenth century. The Prince refers to Queen Victoria's husband, Prince Albert, who had a keen interest in art and sometimes presided at Boards or Committees on artistic matters. *Bal-paré* is French for "a full-dress ball" ; an R.A. is a Royal Academician.

23. LOVE AMONG THE RUINS

WHERE the quiet-coloured end of evening smiles,
    Miles and miles
On the solitary pastures where our sheep
    Half-asleep
Tinkle homeward through the twilight, stray or stop
    As they crop,
Was the site once of a city great and gay,
    So they say,
Of our country's very capital, its prince
    Ages since
Held his court in, gathered councils, wielding far
    Peace or war.

Now, the country does not even boast a tree,
    As you see,
To distinguish slopes of verdure, certain rills
    From the hills
Intersect and give a name to (else they run
    Into one),
Where the domed and daring palace shot its spires
    Up like fires
O'er the hundred-gated circuit of a wall
    Bounding all,
Made of marble, men might march on nor be pressed,
    Twelve abreast.

And such plenty and perfection, see, of grass
    Never was,

Such a carpet as, this summer-time, o'erspreads
    And embeds
Every vestige of the city, guessed alone,
    Stock or stone,
Where a multitude of men breathed joy and woe,
    Long ago ;
Lust of glory pricked their hearts up, dread of shame
    Struck them tame ;
And that glory and that shame alike, the gold
    Bought and sold.

Now, the single little turret that remains
    On the plains,
By the caper overrooted, by the gourd
    Overscored,
While the patching house-leek's head of blossom winks
    Through the chinks,
Marks the basement whence a tower in ancient time
    Sprang sublime,
And a burning ring, all round, the chariots traced
    As they raced,
And the monarch and his minions and his dames
    Viewed the games.

And I know, while thus the quiet-coloured eve
    Smiles to leave
To their folding, all our many-tinkling fleece
    In such peace,
And the slopes and rills in undistinguished grey
    Melt away,

That a girl with eager eyes and yellow hair
 Waits me there
In the turret whence the charioteers caught soul
 For the goal,
When the king looked, where she looks now, breath-
 less, dumb
  Till I come.

But he looked upon the city, every side,
 Far and wide,
All the mountains topped with temples, all the glades'
 Colonnades,
All the causeys, bridges, aqueducts—and then
 All the men.
When I do come, she will speak not, she will stand,
 Either hand
On my shoulder, give her eyes the first embrace
 Of my face,
Ere we rush, ere we extinguish sight and speech
 Each on each.

In one year they sent a million fighters forth
 South and North,
And they built their gods a brazen pillar high
 As the sky,
Yet reserved a thousand chariots in full force—
 Gold, of course.
Oh heart !   Oh blood that freezes, blood that burns !
 Earth's returns
For whole centuries of folly, noise, and sin !
 Shut them in

With their triumphs and their glories and the rest.
  Love is best.

Love among the Ruins is a descriptive lyric built on a
double contrast. There is the contrast between the dim
evening solitude of the green sloping pastures and the
blaring and glaring splendour of the city that once occupied
them. Next there is the contrast between the passing
away of its material pomps and glories—" Gold, of course "
—and the eternity of Love—" Love is best ".

The city that has perished was the brassy capital of some
mighty empire in far-back times ; Browning may have had
memories of the description of the fall of Babylon by the
Greek historian Herodotus. " They " in line 4 of the
second stanza refers to the " slopes of verdure ", which
would " run into one " unless divided by the rivulets.
The lines in the last stanza beginning " Oh heart ! Oh
blood that freezes " mean, " It makes one's blood run hot
and cold to think of the requital that earth has made for
whole centuries of noisy and sinful folly."

24. THE FLOWER'S NAME

HERE's the garden she walked across,
  Arm in my arm, such a short while since :
Hark, now I push its wicket, the moss
  Hinders the hinges and makes them wince.
She must have reached this shrub ere she turned,
  As back with that murmur the wicket swung ;
For she laid the poor snail, my chance foot spurned,
  To feed and forget it the leaves among.

Down this side of the gravel-walk
  She went while her robe's edge brushed the box ;
And here she paused in her gracious talk
  To point me a moth on the milk-white phlox.
Roses, ranged in a valiant row,
  I will never think that she passed you by ;
She loves you noble roses, I know :
  But yonder, see, where the rock-plants lie,

This flower she stopped at, finger on lip,
  Stooped over, in doubt, as settling its claim ;
Till she gave me, with pride to make no slip,
  Its soft meandering Spanish name :
What a name !   Was it love or praise,
  Speech half-asleep or song half-awake ?
I must learn Spanish, one of these days,
  Only for that slow sweet name's sake.

Roses, if I live and do well,
  I may bring her, one of these days,

To fix you fast with as fine a spell,
 Fit you each with his Spanish phrase :
But do not detain me now ; for she lingers
 There, like sunshine over the ground,
And ever I see her soft white fingers
 Searching after the bud she found.

Flower, you Spaniard, look that you grow not,
 Stay as you are and be loved for ever ;
Bud, if I kiss you 'tis that you blow not,
 Mind, the shut pink mouth opens never :
For while it pouts, her fingers wrestle,
 Twinkling the audacious leaves between,
Till round they turn and down they nestle—
 Is not the dear mark still to be seen ?

Where I find her not, beauties vanish ;
 Whither I follow her, beauties flee ;
Is there no method to tell her in Spanish
 June's twice June since she breathed it with me ?
Come, bud, show me the least of her traces,
 Treasure my lady's lightest footfall.
Ah, you may flout and turn up your faces—
 Roses, you are not so fair after all.

The Flower's Name, the other of the " Garden Fancies ",
has the same scene and the same metre as *Sibrandus
Schafnaburgensis*, and no other resemblance. Expressing
sincere passion with a half-wistful, half-impatient playful-
ness, it is perhaps the most completely charming of
Browning's love-lyrics.

" The box " in stanza 2 is the box-wood shrubs that
commonly bordered the gravel paths in Victorian gardens.

sufficient and unique.'' ... so far in the third line refers to the sun, so in the fourth line the phrase 'a world of men'

25. MEETING AT NIGHT

THE grey sea and the long black land ;
And the yellow half-moon large and low ;
And the startled little waves that leap
In fiery ringlets from their sleep,
As I gain the cove with pushing prow
And quench its speed i' the slushy sand.

Then a mile of warm sea-scented beach ;
Three fields to cross till a farm appears ;
A tap at the pane, the quick sharp scratch
And blue spurt of a lighted match,
And a voice less loud, through its joys and fears,
Than the two hearts beating each to each.

PARTING AT MORNING

Round the cape of a sudden came the sea,
And the sun looked over the mountain's rim :
And straight was a path of gold for him,
And the need of a world of men for me.

The impressionistic realism of these two companion-pieces, and the precision of the descriptive touches, as of the little moonlit waves startled by the boat, or the blue spurt of the match, are characteristic of Browning at his best, and have often been praised. He contrasts the moods of the speaker at night and at morning. " *Parting at Morning* ", he said, " is the confession how fleeting is the belief (implied in *Meeting at Night*) that these raptures are self-sufficient and enduring." So *him* in the third line refers to the sun, and the last line means, " I feel the need of returning to my duties in the world of men," or, possibly, " I must now return to the world of men, where my work is needed."

26. A WOMAN'S LAST WORD

Let's contend no more, Love,
  Strive nor weep :
All be as before, Love,
  —Only sleep.

What so wild as words are ?
  I and thou
In debate, as birds are,
  Hawk on bough.

See the creature stalking
  While we speak.
Hush and hide the talking,
  Cheek on cheek.

What so false as truth is,
  False to thee ?
Where the serpent's tooth is
  Shun the tree ;

Where the apple reddens,
  Never pry,
Lest we lose our Edens,
  Eve and I.

Be a god and hold me
  With a charm.
Be a man and fold me
  With thine arm.

Teach me, only teach, Love.
  As I ought
1 will speak thy speech, Love,
  Think thy thought ;

Meet, if thou require it,
  Both demands,
Laying flesh and spirit
  In thy hands.

That shall be to-morrow,
  Not to-night :
1 must bury sorrow
  Out of sight ;

Must a little weep, Love,
  —Foolish me !—
And so fall asleep, Love,
  Loved by thee.

This is a lyric that has met with both ecstatic praise and frigid disapproval. There can be no doubt of the exquisite verse-melody and of the beauty and appropriateness of the metaphors in the opening stanzas. What follows may to modern taste appear sentimental and even mawkish ; but it should be remembered that the poem is a dramatic lyric. Browning is representing, dramatically and perhaps not without a touch of satire, that complete self-surrender to the will of the husband which was at once one of the duties and one of the weapons of much Victorian woman-hood. In another of his poems, *A Lovers' Quarrel*, the woman, after a similar wordy dispute, simply packs up and goes, leaving a discomfited lover only the memories of their happiness together.

The idea in " What so false as truth is, false to thee ? "
is that in intimate relationships factual truth may be
emotionally false ; see Stevenson's essay, *Truth of Inter-
course*, in *Virginibus Puerisque*. What follows means that
the knowledge the woman may gain of her husband from
their quarrel may be dearly bought by the loss of the happiness of her love for him, so that " we lose our Edens, Eve
and I ".

27. ONE WAY OF LOVE

ALL June I bound the rose in sheaves.
Now, rose by rose, I strip the leaves
And strew them where Pauline may pass.
She will not turn aside ?   Alas !
Let them lie.   Suppose they die ?
The chance was they might take her eye.

How many a month I strove to suit
These stubborn fingers to the lute.
To-day I venture all I know.
She will not hear my music ?   So !
Break the string ; fold music's wing :
Suppose Pauline had bade me sing.

My whole life long I learnt to love.
This hour my utmost art I prove
And speak my passion—heaven or hell ?
She will not give me heaven ?   'Tis well !
Lose who may—I still can say,
Those who win heaven, blest are they.

One Way of Love belongs to a group of lyrics in which
the theme is love rejected, and in which the lover accepts
his defeat with dignity and without complaint. The effort
itself is his reward. The sudden blow to the lover's hopes
is admirably reflected in the abrupt change of metrical
movement in the fifth line of each stanza.

28. POETICS

" So say the foolish." Say the foolish so, Love ?
  " Flower she is, my rose," or else, " My very swan
    is she " ;
Or perhaps " Yon maid-moon, blessing earth below,
  Love,
  That art thou "—to them, belike : no such vain
    words from me.

" Hush, rose, blush ; no balm like breath," I chide it :
  " Bend thy neck its best, swan, hers the whiter
    curve."
Be the moon the moon : my Love I place beside it.
  What is she ? Her human self—no lower word will
    serve.

Poetics is included in this selection as an example of the
light and dainty love-lyrics in *Asolando,* Browning's last
volume of poetry. Very probably these were inspired by
his affection for his daughter-in-law, the young American
lady whom his son married in October 1887. The sub-
title of *Asolando* is *Fancies and Facts,* and the theme of
Poetics is that poetical fancies appear foolish in comparison
with the plain truth.

29. HOUSE

SHALL I sonnet-sing you about myself ?
　Do I live in a house you would like to see ?
Is it scant of gear, has it store of pelf ?
　" Unlock my heart with a sonnet-key ? "

Invite the world, as my betters have done ?
　" Take notice : this building remains on view,
Its suites of reception every one,
　Its private apartment and bedroom too ;

For a ticket, apply to the Publisher."
　No : thanking the public, I must decline.
A peep through my window, if folk prefer ;
　But, please you, no foot over threshold of mine !

I have mixed with a crowd and heard free talk
　In a foreign land where an earthquake chanced,
And a house stood gaping, nought to baulk
　Man's eye wherever he gazed or glanced.

The whole of the frontage shaven sheer,
　The inside gaped ; exposed to day,
Right and wrong and common and queer,
　Bare, as the palm of your hand, it lay.

The owner ?　Oh, he had been crushed, no doubt.
　" Odd tables and chairs for a man of wealth !
What a parcel of musty old books about !
　He smoked—no wonder he lost his health.

I doubt if he bathed before he dressed.
  A brasier ?—the pagan, he burned perfumes.
You see it is proved, what the neighbours guessed,
  His wife and himself had separate rooms."

Friends, the goodman of the house at least
  Kept house to himself till an earthquake came :
'Tis the fall of its frontage permits you feast
  On the inside arrangement you praise or blame.

Outside should suffice for evidence :
  And whoso desires to penetrate
Deeper, must dive by the spirit-sense—
  No optics like yours, at any rate !

" Hoity-toity !   A street to explore,
  Your house the exception !   ' *With this same key
Shakespeare unlocked his heart* ', once more."
  Did Shakespeare ?   If so, the less Shakespeare he.

In this provocative poem Browning, by means of the metaphor of the privacy of the home, asserts his determination to keep his inner life sacred from inquisitive prying. It should be only by the exercise of " the spirit sense ", imaginative intuition, that his readers may divine his own personal feelings and opinions. This is an attitude that might be expected from the author of dramatic lyrics and monologues, but in fact Browning has revealed himself very fully in his works, and has permitted many " a peep through my window ".

Many poets have used the sonnet to express their most intimate feelings. Browning makes particular reference to the beginning of Wordsworth's sonnet on the Sonnet, which runs :

> Scorn not the Sonnet ; Critic, you have frowned
> Mindless of its just honours ; with this key
> Shakespeare unlocked his heart ; the melody
> Of this small lute gave ease to Petrarch's wound.

In his last stanza Browning imagines objectors saying, " Other poets have revealed themselves in sonnets ; are you going to be the exception ? Remember once more that the sonnet was the key with which Shakespeare unlocked his heart." " It is highly doubtful ", is Browning's reply, " whether Shakespeare really did so, but if he did, it was unworthy of him."

30. EPILOGUE TO *ASOLANDO*

AT the midnight in the silence of the sleep-time,
    When you set your fancies free,
Will they pass to where—by death, fools think,
      imprisoned—
Low he lies who once so loved you, whom you loved
      so,
    —Pity me ?

Oh to love so, be so loved, yet so mistaken !
    What had I on earth to do
With the slothful, with the mawkish, the unmanly ?
Like the aimless, helpless, hopeless, did I drivel
    —Being—who ?

One who never turned his back but marched breast
    forward,
    Never doubted clouds would break,
Never dreamed, though right were worsted, wrong
      would triumph,
Held we fall to rise, are baffled to fight better,
    Sleep to wake.

No, at noonday in the bustle of man's work-time
    Greet the unseen with a cheer ;
Bid him forward, breast and back as either should be,
" Strive and thrive ", cry, " speed, fight on, fare ever
    There as here."

Browning's *Epilogue* to *Asolando* and Tennyson's *Crossing the Bar*, the almost equally famous but characteristically very different swan-songs of the two greatest Victorian poets, appeared in the same year, 1889. Fortunately ignoring what he had said in *House*, Browning here writes a personal lyric addressed to his most intimate friends. He looked upon death as the prelude to renewed activity of the soul in a future existence. " Without death," he once exclaimed, " which is our churchyardy crape-like word for change, for growth, there could be no prolongation of that which we call life. Never say of me that I am dead."

So the general meaning of the poem is, " When you think of me after I am dead do not pity me—that would be a mistaken return for our mutual love. I was ever active, courageous, and hopeful ; when I am no longer to be seen in this world think of me as still striving and thriving in immortal life, and give me, not pity, but a cheer of encouragement."

Not long before he died Browning read the poem to his son and his daughter-in-law, and said of the third stanza, " It almost sounds like bragging to say this, and as if I ought to cancel it ; but it's the simple truth, and as it's true, it shall stand."

SHORT BIBLIOGRAPHY

THE standard edition of the works of Browning is *The Complete Poetical Works of Robert Browning*, New Edition with Additional Poems first published in 1914, one volume, edited by Augustine Birrell. Macmillan, New York, 1915.

In Everyman's Library, *Poems and Plays by Robert Browning*, 2 vols., nos. 41, 42, contains most of his best and most readable works.

The following books on Browning should be in every school library:

E. Dowden, *Life of Robert Browning*. Originally published in 1904, and reprinted as no. 701 in Everyman's Library.

G. K. Chesterton, *Robert Browning*. English Men of Letters Series. Macmillan, 1903.

Betty Miller, *Robert Browning, a Portrait*. Murray, 1952. Penguin Books, 1958.

Clifford Bax, *The Poetry of the Brownings*. Muller, 1947.

A University Library should also contain:

Letters of Robert Browning and Elizabeth Barrett Browning, 2 vols. Smith, Elder and Co., 1899.

Mrs. Sutherland Orr, *Life and Letters of Robert Browning*, revised by F. G. Kenyon. Murray, 1908.

Letters of Robert Browning, ed. T. L. Hood. Murray, 1933.

De Vane, *A Browning Handbook*. Crofts, 1940.

INDEX OF FIRST LINES

All June I bound the rose in sheaves - - - 112
At the midnight in the silence of the sleep-time - 117

Boot, saddle, to horse, and away! - - - 3

Had I but plenty of money, money enough and to
    spare - - - - - - - - 89
Hamelin Town's in Brunswick - - - - 20
Here's a story shall stir you. Stand up, Greeks dead
    and gone - - - - - - - 17
Here's the garden she walked across. - - - 105

I could have painted pictures like that youth's - 76
I sprang to the stirrup, and Joris, and he - - 5
I've a Friend, over the sea - - - - - 94
It once might have been, once only - - - 97
It was roses, roses, all the way - - - - 58

Just for a handful of silver he left us - - - 60

Kentish Sir Byng stood for his King - - - 1
King Charles, and who'll do him right now? - 2

Let's contend no more, Love - - - - 109
Let us begin and carry up this corpse - - - 62

My first thought was, he lied in every word - - 39

Now that I, tying thy glass mask tightly - - 49

Oh Galuppi, Baldassaro, this is very sad to find - 80
Oh, to be in England - - - - - - 85
On the sea and at the Hogue, sixteen hundred
    ninety-two - - - - - - - 9

Plague take all your pedants, say I   -   -   -   35

Round the cape of a sudden came the sea.   -   -   107

Shall I sonnet-sing you about myself   -   -   -   114
" So say the foolish."   Say the foolish so, Love? -   113

That's my last Duchess painted on the wall -   -   52
The grey sea and the long black land -   -   -   107
The rain set early in to-night   -   -   -   -   55

Vanity, saith the preacher, vanity !   -   -   -   70

What, he on whom our voices unanimously ran   -   32
Where the quiet-coloured end of evening smiles   -   101

Your ghost will walk, you lover of trees   -   -   86